Witchcraft for Beginners

9 EASY PRACTICES IN WHITE MAGIC TO BUILD
LOVING RELATIONSHIPS, DEEPEN YOUR FAITH AND
MANIFEST ABUNDANCE

R. M. JACK

Contents

Introduction

Let me take you back to a moment when everything changed for me. I was in a tiny shop that smelled like lavender and old books. It was tucked away on a quiet street, the kind you might walk past a dozen times without noticing. But that day, I noticed. And thank the heavens I did. Inside, I found a worn copy of a book on white witchcraft. It was as if the universe gave me a little nudge and said, "This is what you need." I dove into the pages, not knowing that this encounter would transform my life.

As I know it to be now, white witchcraft isn't about pointy hats and bubbling cauldrons. It's about positivity, love, and harmony. The kind of magic that celebrates life and all the beauty in it. It's about using natural elements like herbs and crystals to bring peace and joy. And let's clear up a common misconception right now: white magic is as far from sinister as a fluffy white kitten napping in a sunbeam.

Now, here's where things get interesting. White witchcraft doesn't clash with major world religions. In fact, it dances beautifully with Judaism, Christianity, Buddhism, and Hinduism.

How is that possible, you ask? Because at its heart, white witch-craft is all about love. Love for yourself, for others, and for the divine. This book will guide you through these intersections, showing you how magic and faith can coexist in harmony.

Love is the secret sauce of white witchcraft. It's the powerful force that makes the spells work and the rituals meaningful. When you practice with love, you create a ripple effect that touches everyone around you. Imagine a world where more love exists because we dared to share a little more of it. Sounds dreamy, right?

So, what's this book all about? It's your guide to weaving white magic into your everyday life. It's about making your relation-ships sparkle, deepening your connection with God, and enhancing your overall quality of life. We'll explore tools and practices like herbs, crystals, and rituals. You'll learn how to use them to invite love, happiness, and abundance into your life.

And here's the exciting part: we present nine simple, essential practices that are incredibly simple to learn and implement in your daily life. You may be thinking, are there only nine prac-tices? No certainly, there are far more than nine but this distilla-tion was deliberate. We want to make your entry into your own magical journey as easy as possible and, most of all, allow you to chart your own course from the end of this book onward. Philosophically, we also don't want you to be overburdened by some teachers who feel that they know where your journey should go better than you do. The lessons are designed to guide you step by step into a life filled with love, positivity and joy. Think of it as a journey where each day brings you closer to the extraordinary life you deserve.

But let's address the elephant in the room. Witchcraft has a bit of a reputation problem, doesn't it? There are myths and misconceptions galore. This book sets the record straight with a respectful, stress-free approach to integrating these practices into your life. You'll see that it's about spiritual growth and empowerment, not about waving a wand and expecting miracles.

As you turn these pages, I invite you to open your mind and heart. You're embarking on a journey of discovery, and I'm right here with you. Consider this book your supportive guide, a friend who's walked this path and is eager to share what they've learned.

I am thrilled to share this journey with you. My own path has been filled with surprises, revelations, and a lot of love. You're not alone in this. You're joining a growing community of people who are finding their magic and making the world a better place, one spell at a time. So, are you ready to start your magical adventure? Let's do this together.

CHAPTER 1

Understanding the Foundations of White Witchcraft

Y ou know those moments when you're convinced the universe is whispering secrets just to you? Like the time you randomly picked up a book in a quiet corner of a library, and it turned out to be exactly what you needed? That's how I stumbled upon white witchcraft. It felt like a cosmic nudge, a wink from the universe saying, "Hey, there's more to life than meets the eye." That first encounter was the beginning of a path that's brought more clarity, love, and joy into my life than I ever thought possible. And now, here we are, about to dive into the fascinating world of white witchcraft—a world that's all about benevolence, positivity, and a touch of magic in everyday life.

1.1 THE ESSENCE OF WHITE MAGIC IN MODERN LIFE

Let's start with a little history lesson, shall we? But don't worry, this isn't the snooze-fest you remember from high school. White magic has been around for ages, kind of like that wise old grandfather figure who's seen it all and offers nuggets of wisdom when you most need them. Historically, white magic has been about improving the world, focusing on healing, protection, and positive transformation. You see, while black magic might have that reputation for being all doom and gloom, white magic is its benevolent counterpart. Imagine it as the friendly neighbor who always has a smile and a plate of cookies, ready to help you out.

In ancient civilizations—think Egypt, Rome, and Greece—magic was as normal as your morning cup of coffee, intertwined with religion and science. It wasn't about casting spells willy-nilly but about a deeper understanding of the world and our place in it. Key figures like Thoth (or Hermes, if you're feeling Roman) were seen as patrons of learning and magic, because white magic is all about knowledge and self-improvement. It's like a self-help book with a magical twist.

Fast forward to today, and you might be wondering, "How does this ancient stuff fit into my modern life?" Well, my friend, white magic is more relevant than ever. In a world buzzing with stress and disconnectedness, white magic offers a way to find balance and well-being. Think of it as a toolkit for mental wellness. You can use simple practices like meditation or creating a small ritual with herbs and crystals to ground yourself. It's about creating moments of peace in our hectic lives—a little oasis of calm in the chaos.

But here's the thing about magic: it's not just about waving a wand and hoping for the best. Ethical considerations are at the core of white witchcraft. It's like the golden rule with a bit of sparkle. The idea is to practice magic with intention and consent, always mindful of the impact on others and the environment. Magic isn't a free-for-all; it's a responsibility.

Now, let's chat about something that might surprise you—technology in magic. Yes, you heard that right. In our digital age, technology can be a fantastic ally in your magical practice. From digital tools that help you track your spells to online communities that offer support and guidance, technology brings a new dimension to the practice. It's like having a coven in your pocket, ready to offer insights and encouragement whenever you need it. You can even use apps for meditation or astrology to enhance your practice, all without losing the essence of tradition.

In essence, white magic is about weaving a little more positivity and intention into your life. It's about connecting with the world around you, finding peace in the everyday, and embracing the magic that exists all around us. Whether you're using herbs to brew a calming tea or connecting with like-minded souls online, white magic is a practice that's as ancient as it is modern, offering timeless wisdom wrapped in a 21st-century package.

1.2 LOVE AS A UNIVERSAL POWER IN WITCHCRAFT

Let's face it, love is the stuff that makes life worth living. It's the warm hug on a cold day, the laughter shared with friends, and the quiet moments of peace when you know you're exactly where you're meant to be. In white witchcraft, love isn't just a nice-to-have; it's the very heartbeat of the practice. Love drives intentions and shapes outcomes, making it the transformative energy that fuels magical work. Think of love as the magical yeast that makes everything rise. Without it, nothing quite turns out as it should. When you infuse your magical practices with love, you're adding a powerful ingredient that amplifies everything else. It's like adding a double shot of espresso to your morning coffee—a little extra oomph that makes all the difference.

Love connects with natural and supernatural elements in ways that are both subtle and profound. Picture this: you're holding a rose quartz crystal, known for its love-enhancing properties. You close your eyes and focus on the warmth radiating from the stone, letting it fill you with a sense of peace and compassion. That's love at work, linking you to the energy of the universe. Or imagine crafting a simple love spell using herbs like lavender and rosemary. These aren't just random plants; they're chosen for their specific properties that resonate with love and healing. When you combine these elements, you're tapping into a network of energies that boost your intentions and bring your desires closer to reality. It's a bit like cooking—using the right ingredients can turn a simple dish into something truly magical.

Now, I'm sure you've heard the saying that you can't pour from an empty cup. In white witchcraft, self-love is the foundation of all magical work. It's about recognizing your own worth and treating yourself with kindness and respect. Self-love rituals can be as simple as a daily affirmation or as elaborate as a personal ceremony under the moonlight. When you love yourself, you empower your magical abilities, making your spells more effective and your intentions clearer. But it doesn't stop there. Love for others is equally important, and magic offers unique ways to heal and strengthen relationships. Whether it's mending a rift with a friend or deepening your connection with a partner, using magic to share love can bring about profound healing and understanding.

One of the most beautiful aspects of love in witchcraft is its expansive nature. Love isn't meant to be hoarded or hidden away; it's meant to be shared. When you engage in group rituals focused on community love, you're contributing to a collective pool of positive energy that benefits everyone involved. It's a bit like throwing a pebble into a pond—the ripples spread far and wide, touching lives in ways you might never see. Love-based meditation practices are another way to share this energy, allowing you to connect with others on a spiritual level and create a sense of unity. Imagine a group of people sitting in a circle, eyes closed, hearts open, all focusing on sending love out into the world. It's a powerful image and an even more powerful practice.

Try This: Love-Inspired Ritual

- Who: Yourself or a small group of friends
- What: A simple ritual to share love and positive energy
- Where: A quiet room or outdoor space
- When: Anytime you feel the need to connect and share love
- Why: To amplify love and spread positive energy

1. Gather a few items that symbolize love for you—perhaps a rose quartz crystal, a pink candle, or some dried rose petals.
2. Arrange these items in a small circle and sit comfortably around them.
3. Close your eyes and take a few deep breaths, centering yourself.
4. Visualize love as a warm, golden light filling your heart.
5. Imagine this light expanding, filling the room, and reaching out to everyone participating.
6. Sit in this shared energy for as long as it feels right, then gently bring yourself back, opening your eyes and sharing a smile with those around you.

Love is a living, breathing force in white witchcraft. It's the gentle nudge that guides your intentions and the fierce power that helps them come to life. When you embrace love in your practice, you're not just making magic—you're making a difference in the world.

1.3 ALIGNING WITCHCRAFT WITH YOUR FAITH

If you've ever thought that witchcraft and traditional religion were like oil and water, forever destined to stay apart, you're in for a delightful surprise. White witchcraft can cozy up with major world religions like Judaism, Christianity, Buddhism, and Hinduism, each sharing a mutual respect and reverence for the divine. Let's look at Judaism, where the sanctity of nature plays a crucial role. There's a beautiful connection between the Jewish reverence for the natural world and the witch's practice of drawing power from the earth. Picture a Jewish family gathered around their Shabbat table, the flicker of candlelight reflecting the same awe and respect for creation that a witch feels when crafting a spell under the full moon.

In Christianity, the relationship is a bit of a tangled web. But take a closer look, and you'll see that prayer is a common thread that weaves both practices together. Christian prayers can find their way into rituals, offering a sense of comfort and familiarity. Imagine creating a ritual where you light a candle, recite a psalm, and let the warmth of those ancient words infuse your intentions. It's about finding the sacred in the ordinary and letting it guide your magical work.

Buddhism brings mindfulness to the table—a practice that pairs beautifully with spellcasting. It's all about being present, aware, and intentional. When you cast a spell with the mindfulness of a Buddhist monk, you're not just going through the motions. You're engaging with every element, every word, every intention. It's about feeling the energy shift around you as you focus your mind and spirit on your magical goals.

Then there's Hinduism, with its deep respect for all life forms. This respect aligns seamlessly with the witch's ethos of doing no harm and living in harmony with all beings. Imagine performing a ritual to honor the spirits of the earth, channeling the same reverence found in Hindu practices. It's about acknowledging the interconnectedness of life and letting that awareness shape your magical work.

Prayer and intention are like the dynamic duo of white witchcraft, each strengthening your connection with the divine. Whether you're incorporating a prayer before casting a spell or using religious texts as a source of inspiration, these practices remind us that magic is as much about the heart as it is about the hands. A prayer-infused ritual can be as simple as saying a few words of gratitude before lighting a candle or as elaborate as crafting a full ceremony around a sacred text. It's about creating a dialogue with the divine and letting that conversation guide your magic.

Respect for all beliefs is a cornerstone of white witchcraft. It's about understanding that everyone walks their own path and that each path has value. In magical communities that thrive best with love and harmony, inclusivity is key. It's like hosting a potluck where everyone brings their unique dish to the table, creating a feast of diverse flavors and experiences. Most of the Hindus attending will not eat the beef dishes, but the rest of the participants will be there to respect that choice and to embrace the diversity of one another's views. By embracing different spiritual perspectives, you enrich your practice and open yourself to new ways of thinking and being.

Creating personalized practices is where the magic truly happens. Tailor your spells and rituals to align with your personal faith, choosing symbols that resonate with your spiritual beliefs. Maybe it's incorporating a cross into your altar setup or using a lotus flower to represent rebirth and enlightenment. These choices make your practice uniquely yours, a reflection of your beliefs and goals.

Exercise: Creating Your Personalized Ritual

- Who: Yourself
- What: A ritual that aligns with your spiritual beliefs
- Where: A quiet space where you feel comfortable
- When: Any time you feel called to connect with your faith and magic
- Why: To create a practice that reflects your unique spiritual journey

1. Choose a symbol or object that represents your faith— perhaps a picture, small figure, or a sacred text.
2. Place this symbol in the center of your ritual space.
3. Light a candle or incense to signify the beginning of your ritual.
4. Spend a few moments in silent reflection or prayer, focusing on your intentions and the energy you wish to manifest.
5. Conclude your ritual with an expression of gratitude, either silently or spoken aloud.

This ritual is just a starting point. As you continue to explore the intersections of witchcraft and faith, you'll find new ways to deepen your connection with the divine. Remember, the heart of witchcraft is not about following a set of rigid rules. It's about embracing the journey, finding your truth, and letting your personal magic shine.

1.4 THE ROLE OF INTENTIONAL LIVING IN MAGIC

Imagine your life as a beautiful canvas, each stroke of paint representing a choice, a moment, or an intention. In the world of white witchcraft, living with intention is like choosing your colors with care, creating a masterpiece that reflects your deepest desires and values. It's about moving through life with a sense of meaning and purpose, ensuring that your magical practices and everyday actions align with who you truly are. It's a shift into taking personal responsibility for your life, rather than letting life happen to you, you become the artist, shaping your reality with clarity and focus. This concept of intentional living transforms each ritual into a powerful act of self-expression and growth, as you set clear intentions that guide your actions and thoughts.

Setting clear, focused intentions is the cornerstone of effective magical practice. It's like using a GPS to navigate your way through the mystical landscape of life. Without clear intentions, your magic might feel scattered, like a puzzle missing a few crucial pieces. Picture yourself standing before an altar, the flickering candlelight reflecting your hopes and dreams. As you prepare for a ritual, take a moment to breathe deeply and focus on what you truly want to manifest. Whether it's inner peace, abundance, or healing, define your intention with precision. This clarity acts as a beacon, guiding your energy and ensuring your magic hits its mark.

But intentionality isn't just for the magical moments. It spills over into everyday life, turning routine actions into opportunities for mindfulness and growth. Consider the simple act of making your morning coffee. Instead of a mindless chore, approach it as a ritual. As you measure the beans and pour the water, infuse each step with gratitude and intention. Let the aroma awaken your senses and remind you of the beauty in the mundane. When you live intentionally, even the smallest actions become imbued with meaning, creating a ripple effect that enhances your entire day.

Mindfulness and magic are best friends, each continually strengthening the other. When you incorporate mindfulness techniques into your magical practice, you sharpen your focus and clarity, making your spells more effective. Before starting your spellwork, take a few minutes for mindful meditation. Close your eyes, breathe deeply, and allow your thoughts to settle and quiet your mind. In this quiet space, visualize your intention as a vibrant light, growing stronger with each breath. This practice not only centers your mind but also aligns your energy with your goals, setting the stage for powerful manifestation.

Journaling is another tool that supports intentional living and magic. It's like having a conversation with your inner self, exploring your thoughts and intentions on paper. After a ritual, take some time to reflect on your experiences. Write down what you hoped to achieve, how you felt during the process, and any insights that surfaced. This practice not only reinforces your intentions but also provides a valuable record of your growth and progress. The shear act of putting pen to paper also helps you consciously distill your thoughts more fully and with better accuracy. Over time, your journal becomes a treasure trove of wisdom, offering guidance and inspiration whenever you need it.

Aligning your intentions with your values is key to creating magic that resonates with your true self. It's about choosing spells and rituals that reflect your personal and spiritual beliefs, ensuring your practice remains authentic and meaningful. Start by setting values-based goals that guide your magical work. Ask yourself what you stand for, what you hope to achieve, and how your magic can support these aspirations. When your intentions are rooted in your values, your magic flows naturally, enhancing your life in ways that feel right and true. By seeing your results improve during this process, your confidence will grow and your ability to expand your skills will grow as well.

Creating routines that foster intentionality is like setting the rhythm of your life to a melody that uplifts and inspires. Establish morning rituals that set a positive tone for the day, such as a few moments of meditation or a simple affirmation. As the sun sets, engage in evening reflections to assess your progress and realign your intentions. This practice not only keeps you grounded but also reinforces your commitment to living with purpose and intention. Through these routines, you cultivate a way of being that supports your magical practice and personal growth, turning each day into a dance of intention and possibility.

1.5 BUILDING A SACRED SPACE FOR PRACTICE

Imagine coming home after a long day, kicking off your shoes, and stepping into your own little slice of serenity—a sacred space just for you. Creating such a space isn't just about aesthetics; it's about crafting a personal sanctuary where magic thrives and distractions melt away. This is where your focus sharpens and distractions and everyday noise takes a backseat. A dedicated sacred space brings a sense of calm and clarity, both physically and mentally. Think of it as your personal retreat from the chaos of the world, a place where you can recharge and reconnect with your inner self. It's like having a little oasis where the outside world doesn't intrude, where you can breathe deeply and just be.

So how do you go about setting up this magical haven? First, you need to find the perfect spot. Look for a place that feels right to you, whether it's a cozy corner of your living room, a nook in your bedroom, or even a spot in your garden if you're feeling adventurous. Remember, it doesn't have to be a big space; it just needs to feel right. Once you've chosen your location, it's time to gather your essential tools and decorations.

Think about what inspires you and fills you with a sense of peace. Perhaps it's a collection of crystals, a few candles, or some cherished mementos. These items don't just serve as decorations; they become focal points for your practice, grounding you and enhancing the sacredness of your space.

Nature plays a vital role in any sacred space. Incorporating elements of the natural world not only enhances the magic but also deepens your connection to the earth. Consider adding plants that thrive indoors, like succulents or ferns, that bring a touch of life and vitality to your space. Stones and crystals can also add their unique energies, grounding and amplifying your intentions. Don't forget about the power of natural light and fresh air. If possible, choose a spot with a window that allows sunlight to stream in, filling the space with warmth and energy. When the weather permits, throw open the windows and let the fresh air cleanse and rejuvenate your sacred space. It's amazing how much difference a bit of nature can make, transforming an ordinary area into a magical sanctuary. Be sure to remove any and all electronics, even your mobile phone so you reduce your temptations to let distractions into your sacred space.

Maintaining the energy and sanctity of your sacred space is just as important as creating it. Regular cleansing rituals help keep the energy fresh and inviting. Whether it's smudging with sage, ringing a bell, or using a favorite essential oil, these practices clear away any stagnant or negative energy, leaving your space vibrant and welcoming. Consider personalizing your space with seasonal updates to keep it alive and attuned to the natural cycles of the world. Maybe a small pumpkin in the fall or fresh flowers in the spring—these little touches keep your space dynamic and aligned with the ever-changing world around you.

Reflect and Refresh: Sacred Space Maintenance

- Who: Yourself
- What: A simple ritual to cleanse and refresh your sacred space
- Where: Your chosen sacred space
- When: At the start of each new season or whenever you feel the energy needs a boost
- Why: To maintain a vibrant and welcoming space

1. Begin by gathering your cleansing tools—perhaps a sage smudge stick, a small bell, or some essential oils.
2. Stand in your space, take a deep breath, and focus on your intention to clear and refresh the energy.
3. Use your cleansing tool to move through the space, paying attention to corners and areas that may feel stagnant.
4. As you cleanse, visualize any negative energy dissipating, leaving your space filled with light and positivity.
5. Conclude with a moment of gratitude, acknowledging your sacred space as a source of strength and peace.

Creating and maintaining a sacred space is a powerful practice that supports your magical work and personal growth. It becomes a reflection of your journey, evolving with you as you continue to explore the vast and wondrous world of white witchcraft. As you spend time in this space, you'll find your focus sharpening, your heart opening, and your magic flourishing. It's your personal corner of the universe, dedicated to nurturing your spirit and celebrating the magic in your life.

1.6 THE NINE ESSENTIALS

Here are the top nine spells, rituals, and exercises of white magic to help manifest your desired outcomes:

- **Candle Magic:** Use colored candles corresponding to your intention (e.g., green for prosperity, pink for love) and focus on your goal while lighting the candle.
- **Gratitude Decanter:** Write down things you are grateful for on slips of paper and place them in a decanter. This keeps your energy positive and open to receiving more.
- **Nature Ritual:** Spend time in nature, connecting with its energy, and visualize your intentions while grounding yourself.
- **Mirror Work:** Stand in front of a mirror, affirming your desires and visualizing them as already achieved to boost your confidence and manifest positivity.
- **Money Magnet Spell:** Place coins in a bowl with herbs like basil and cinnamon to attract wealth, focusing on your intention each day.
- **Full Moon Ritual:** Use the energy of the full moon to release what no longer serves you and set your intentions for the coming cycle.
- **Vision Board:** Create a visual representation of your goals using images and words that resonate with what you want to manifest.
- **Crystal Programming:** Choose crystals that resonate with your goals, hold them in your hands, and clearly state your intention to program them with your energy.
- **Affirmation Practice:** Regularly recite positive affirmations that align with your goals to rewire your mindset and attract your desires.

1.7 CANDLE MAGIC

Candle magic is a beautiful and accessible practice within white witchcraft, offering a gentle way to manifest your deepest desires for love, spirituality, and personal growth. It's a heartfelt ritual that connects you with the energies around you, allowing you to focus your intentions and invite positive changes into your life.

1. Choosing the Right Candle Colors:

The color of the candle plays a significant role in your ritual, as each hue resonates with specific energies:

- Love: Opt for pink, for affection and harmony, or red, for passion and romance. These colors will help attract loving energies into your life.
- Spirituality: White is the go-to color for spiritual work, representing purity, clarity, and connection to the divine. It can also amplify the effects of other colors.
- Manifestation: Green symbolizes abundance and prosperity, while yellow can infuse clarity and confidence into your intentions.

2. Preparing Your Sacred Space:

Creating a serene and sacred environment is crucial. Find a quiet, comfortable place where you can focus without distractions. Cleanse the space with sage or salt, inviting positive energies and setting a peaceful tone for your practice. Be sure to find your sage from a source that is clean, pure and uncontaminated. You can set up your space with your chosen candle, any crystals that resonate with your intentions, and a piece of paper on which you write your goals.

3. Setting Your Intention:

Before you light the candle, take a moment to hold it in your hands. Breathe deeply and visualize your desired outcome. Feel the emotions associated with achieving your goal, whether it's the warmth of love, the light of spiritual clarity, or the joy of manifesting abundance. You might also choose to carve symbols or words into the candle, such as hearts for love or the word "abundance" to focus your intentions.

4. Lighting the Candle:

As you light the candle, speak your intention aloud or in your mind. This moment is sacred, as you're sending your desires into the universe. You may recite a specific affirmation that resonates with your goals, such as "I welcome love into my life" or "I attract abundance effortlessly." Feel the warmth of the flame and allow it to represent the spark of your desires taking flight.

5. Focusing on the Flame:

While the candle burns, sit quietly and focus on the flame. Visualize your intention as if it has already come true. Picture the love you desire, the spiritual growth you seek, and the life you plan to build.

6. Closing the Ritual:

After reflecting on your notes, thank the universe for the blessings you've received and express your openness to receive each.

1.8 GRATITUDE DECANTER

The gratitude decanter is a heartfelt and meaningful tool used in white witchcraft that can help you cultivate a deeper sense of love, spirituality, and manifestation in your life. It's a beautiful practice that encourages mindfulness and appreciation, allowing you to focus on the positive aspects of your life while attracting even more blessings.

1. The Purpose of the Gratitude Decanter:

At its core, the gratitude decanter is a tangible reminder of all the good things in your life. By acknowledging and appreciating these moments, you raise your vibrational frequency, which in turn aligns you with the energies of love, abundance, and spiritual growth. This practice encourages a mindset of positivity and opens your heart to receive even more.

2. How to Create Your Gratitude Decanter:

- Gather Your Materials: Choose a decanter that resonates with you; it can be a beautiful glass decanter, an old mason jar, or any container that feels special. You'll also need small slips of paper and a pen.
- Set Your Intentions: Before you begin, take a moment to set your intentions for the decanter. You might state something like, "This decanter will hold my gratitude and attract more love, abundance, and spiritual insight into my life."

3. Writing Your Gratitude Notes:

Whenever you experience something you are grateful for—no matter how big or small—write it down on a slip of paper and place it in the decanter. For love, you might write about moments you cherish with loved ones, while for spirituality, jot down experiences that brought you peace or enlightenment. For manifestation, note any progress you make toward your goals.

4. Regular Practice:

Make it a habit to add to your gratitude decanter regularly. You might choose to do this daily, weekly, or whenever you have an inspiration. Reflecting on your blessings helps reinforce a positive mindset and reminds you of the good in your life.

5. Celebrating Your Gratitude:

Periodically, perhaps at the end of each month or during a full moon, take some time to sit with your gratitude decanter. Read through the notes and allow yourself to feel the joy and appreciation for all that you have. This practice not only reinforces feelings of love and abundance but also serves as a powerful manifestation tool, and to remind you to be consciously clear about what you want to attract in your life.

6. Closing the Ritual:

After reflecting on your notes, thank the universe for the blessings you've received and express your openness to receive each.

1.9 NATURE RITUAL

The nature ritual is a beautiful practice in white witchcraft that allows you to connect deeply with the natural world while focusing on your goals of love, spirituality, and manifestation. Engaging with nature can be profoundly healing and inspiring, as it reminds us of the interconnectedness of all life and the energy that surrounds us. Here's how to perform a nature ritual that honors these intentions.

1. Choosing Your Location:

Select a serene outdoor space that feels special to you—this could be a quiet park, a forest, a beach, or even your backyard. The key is to find a place where you feel at peace and can connect with the natural elements around you.

2. Preparing Yourself:

Before you begin, take a moment to ground yourself. You can do this by taking a few deep breaths, feeling your feet on the earth, and tuning into the sounds and sensations of nature. This helps you center your energy and open your heart.

3. Setting Your Intentions:

As you prepare for your ritual, clearly state your intentions. You might say something like, "I am open to receiving love," "I seek spiritual growth," or "I attract abundance into my life." Visualize these goals manifesting as you speak them, allowing your feelings to resonate with the energy of nature.

4. Connecting with Nature:

Engage with the elements around you. You might walk barefoot on the grass, touch the bark of a tree, or listen to the sounds of birds. Mindfully, acknowledge the beauty and wisdom of nature, allowing it to inspire and uplift you. You can also gather natural items like leaves, stones, or flowers that resonate with your intentions.

5. Performing Your Ritual:

You may want to create a small, personal space using the natural items you collected. Arrange them in a way that feels meaning-ful, and take a moment to express gratitude for the earth and its gifts. You can also light a candle or incense to represent your intentions if you wish to incorporate a small flame. Sit quietly, close your eyes, and visualize what achieving your goals looks and feels like. Imagine love flowing into your life, spiritual insights illuminating your path, or abundance surrounding you. Embrace the feelings of gratitude and joy as if your desires are already manifesting.

6. Closing the Ritual:

When you feel ready, take a moment to thank nature for its energy and support.

2.0 MIRROR WORK

The mirror work ritual is a transformative practice that allows you to connect with your inner self while focusing on your goals of love, spirituality, and manifestation. This ritual encourages self-reflection and self-acceptance, helping you to cultivate a deeper sense of worthiness and openness to receive the love and abundance you seek.

1. Preparing Your Space:

Find a quiet, comfortable space where you can place a mirror at eye level. This can be a handheld mirror, a wall mirror, or even a compact mirror—whatever feels right for you. Ensure the area is well-lit and free from distractions, allowing you to focus entirely on yourself.

2. Setting Your Intention:

Before beginning, take a moment to center yourself. Close your eyes, take a few deep breaths, and think about what you want to achieve. Whether it's attracting love, enhancing your spiritual practice, or manifesting your goals, clearly state your intention. You might say, "I am open to giving and receiving love," or "I am ready to embrace my spiritual journey."

3. Engaging with Your Reflection:

Once you feel grounded, open your eyes and gaze into the mirror. Look deeply into your own eyes, acknowledging yourself with love and compassion. This connection is essential, as it allows you to confront any negative beliefs or self-doubt that may be holding you back.

4. Affirmations and Self-Love:

Begin to recite affirmations that align with your intentions. For love, you might say, "I am deserving of love and kindness." For spirituality, you could affirm, "I am connected to the universe and my faith and open to its guidance." For manifestation, consider saying, "I attract abundance effortlessly." As you speak these affirmations, feel the energy of the words resonating within you, and allow yourself to accept the truth of what you are saying.

5. Visualizing Your Goals:

As you continue to look into the mirror, visualize your intentions as if they have already come to fruition. Picture yourself surrounded by love, experiencing spiritual growth, or achieving your goals. Embrace the feelings of joy, gratitude, and fulfillment that accompany these visualizations.

6. Closing the Ritual:

Once you feel complete with your affirmations and visualizations, take a moment to thank yourself for this time of self-reflection and growth. Gently smile at your reflection, acknowledging the beautiful soul that you are.

2.1 MONEY MAGNET

The money magnet ritual focuses on attracting financial abundance and prosperity into your life. While its primary goal is to create a flow of abundance, it can also be intertwined with intentions for love and spirituality, as financial security can enhance your overall well-being and allow you to pursue your spiritual journey with greater freedom.

1. Gathering Your Materials:

To perform this ritual, you will need a few simple items:

- A green candle: Green represents abundance and prosperity.
- A small bowl of salt: Salt is used for purification and protection.
- Cinnamon: This spice is known for its properties of attraction and prosperity.
- Coins or small bills: These can symbolize the wealth you wish to attract.
- A piece of paper and pen: For writing down your intentions.

2. Creating Your Sacred Space:

Cleanse your sacred space by smudging with sage or sprinkling salt around, creating an area filled with positive energy. Arrange your materials in front of you, and light the green candle as you prepare to set your intentions.

3. Setting Your Intentions:

Take a moment to ground yourself. Close your eyes, breathe deeply, and think about what financial abundance means to you. Write down your specific intentions on the piece of paper. For example, you might write, "I am open to receiving financial abundance," or "I attract opportunities for prosperity" or "I have X amount in my bank account." Feel the energy of your words as you write them.

4. Incorporating Cinnamon:

Sprinkle a small amount of cinnamon around the candle and on top of the paper with your intentions. As you do this, visualize the sweet aroma attracting wealth and opportunities into your life. You can say a short affirmation, such as, "As I sprinkle this cinnamon, I attract abundance effortlessly."

5. Visualizing Abundance:

With the candle lit, sit comfortably and focus on the flame. Visualize your intentions coming to fruition. Picture yourself surrounded by financial abundance, feeling secure and free. Allow the feelings of joy and gratitude to fill your heart, embracing the belief that you are worthy of this abundance.

6. Closing the Ritual:

After spending time visualizing, take the coins or bills and hold them in your hands. Imagine the energy of wealth flowing into your life as you express gratitude for the abundance you are attracting.

2.2 FULL MOON

The full moon ritual is a powerful and transformative practice in white witchcraft that harnesses the energy of the full moon, which is a time of heightened intuition, reflection, and manifestation. This ritual serves as a beautiful opportunity to release what no longer serves you and to set intentions for love, spirituality, and abundance.

1. Preparing for the Full Moon:

As the full moon approaches, take time to reflect on what you want to let go of in your life—old patterns, negative beliefs, or anything that hinders your growth. This is also a time to consider what you wish to attract, whether it's love, spiritual insight, or prosperity.

2. Gathering Your Materials:

To perform your full moon ritual, you will need:

- A white or silver candle: Symbolizing purity and the energy of the moon.
- A piece of paper and a pen: For writing down your intentions and what you wish to release.
- A bowl of water: To represent the element of water, which is associated with emotions and intuition.
- Crystals: Such as clear quartz or moonstone, to amplify your intentions.

3. Creating Your Sacred Space:

Find a peaceful area where you can be in tune with the moonlight. Set up your materials, placing the candle and bowl of water on a flat surface. If it's safe, consider performing the ritual outdoors under the moonlight, or by a window where you can see the moon.

4. Setting Your Intentions:

Begin by lighting the candle and taking a few deep breaths to center yourself. Close your eyes and visualize the moon's light surrounding you, filling you with clarity and purpose. Write down what you want to release on one side of the paper and your intentions for love, spirituality, or manifestation on the other side.

5. Releasing and Manifesting:

Once you've written your intentions, burn the paper over the candle flame as a symbolic act of releasing what no longer serves you. As the smoke rises, visualize your old patterns dissolving into the universe. Then, focus on your intentions for love or abundance, feeling the energy of the full moon supporting your desires.

6. Closing the Ritual:

After you have released and set your intentions, take a moment to express gratitude to the moon and the universe for their guidance and support.

2.3 VISION BOARD

The vision board is an empowering practice that helps you visualize and manifest your deepest desires for love, spirituality, and abundance. By creating a visual representation of your goals, you align your energy with what you wish to attract, making it a powerful tool for manifestation.

1. Gathering Your Materials:

To create your vision board, you will need:

- A board: This can be a corkboard, poster board, or even a digital platform if you prefer.

- Magazines, printed images, or art supplies: Collect visuals that resonate with your goals.
- Scissors and glue or tape: For assembling your board.
- Markers or pens: To add words or affirmations that inspire you.

2. Setting Your Intentions:

Before you start, take some time to reflect on what you truly desire in your life. Consider what love means to you, how you wish to grow spiritually, and what abundance looks like for you. Write down these intentions to clarify your goals. This step is essential, as it helps you focus your energy on what you wish to attract.

3. Creating Your Vision Board:

Cut out images, words, and affirmations that resonate with your intentions. For love, you might include pictures of couples, hearts, or quotes about love. For abundance, look for images that represent financial freedom, success, and prosperity. Arrange these elements on your board in a way that feels harmonious and inspiring to you.

4. Infusing Your Board with Energy:

Once your vision board is complete, take a moment to hold it in your hands and close your eyes. Visualize your intentions coming to life as you breathe deeply. Feel the emotions associated with achieving your goals—joy, love, and fulfillment. You might also choose to light a candle or use incense during this process to enhance the energy of your intentions.

5. Displaying Your Vision Board:

Place your vision board somewhere you will see it regularly, such as your bedroom, office, or a special space. This constant reminder will help keep your intentions at the forefront of your mind. As you look at it, take a moment to visualize your goals and feel gratitude for the manifestations that are on their way to you.

6. Regularly Engage with Your Board:

Make it a practice to engage with your board often, preferably daily for a few minutes.

2.4 CRYSTAL PROGRAMMING

The crystal programming ritual is a practice that allows you to imbue your crystals with specific intentions related to love, spirituality, and manifestation. By programming your crystals, you align your faith and positive energy with the natural energy in each crystal, making them powerful allies in your journey.

1. Choosing Your Crystals:

Begin by selecting crystals that resonate with your intentions. For love, consider using rose quartz, known for its ability to attract and foster love and compassion. For spirituality, amethyst can enhance your spiritual growth and intuition. For manifestation, citrine is a wonderful choice, as it is associated with abundance and personal power. Trust your intuition when choosing the crystals that speak to your heart.

2. Cleansing Your Crystals:

Before programming your crystals, it's essential to cleanse them of any previous energies they may hold. You can do this by rinsing them under running water, placing them in moonlight for a night, or smudging them with sage. This step helps create a clear and open channel for your intentions.

3. Setting Your Intentions:

Find a quiet space where you can focus your energy. Hold your chosen crystal in your hands, close your eyes, and take several deep breaths. Visualize your intentions clearly in your mind. For love, imagine the feelings of warmth and connection you wish to attract. For spirituality, visualize the growth and clarity you desire. For manifestation, picture the abundance and opportunities flowing into your life.

4. Programming the Crystal:

Once you feel centered and connected to your intentions, speak them aloud or silently while holding the crystal. You might say something like, "I program this rose quartz to attract and enhance love in my life," or "I imbue this citrine with the energy of abundance and success." Feel the energy of your words resonating through the crystal, and trust that your intentions are being absorbed.

5. Visualizing Your Intentions:

As you speak your intentions, close your eyes and visualize them as if they have already manifested. Feel the joy and gratitude associated with achieving these goals. Allow yourself to bask in these positive emotions, reinforcing the connection between your desires and the crystal's energy.

6. Using Your Crystals:

After programming your crystals, you can incorporate them into your daily life. Carry them in your pocket, or wear them as jewelry.

2.5 AFFIRMATION PRACTICE

The use of the affirmations is deeply transformative. Affirmations are positive statements that help you challenge and overcome self-sabotaging thoughts, allowing you to create a more fulfilling and empowered life. Each must be stated in present tense, positive and personal for the best results.

1. Understanding Affirmations:

Affirmations are simple yet powerful phrases that reflect your desired reality. By repeating these statements, you reprogram your subconscious mind, promoting a more positive and abundant mindset. This practice is especially beneficial for attracting love, enhancing your spiritual journey, and manifesting your goals.

2. Crafting Your Affirmations:

To begin, take some time to reflect on what you truly desire:

- For love: Create affirmations that resonate with your heart, such as "I am worthy of love and attract healthy relationships."
- For spirituality: Consider statements like "I am open to receiving spiritual guidance and insights now."
- For manifestation: Use affirmations like "Abundance flows to me effortlessly, and I am grateful for my opportunities."

3. Setting the Right Environment:

Choose a quiet, comfortable space where you can focus without distractions. This could be a cozy corner in your home, a peaceful outdoor setting, or anywhere that feels nurturing to you. You may want to light a candle or burn incense to create a calming atmosphere that enhances your practice.

4. Repeating Your Affirmations:

Once you've crafted your affirmations, find a time each day to repeat them. You can do this in front of a mirror, allowing yourself to look into your own eyes as you affirm your worth and desires. Alternatively, write them down in a journal, say them aloud, or even record yourself and listen to the affirmations throughout your day. The key is to express them with genuine emotion and conviction.

5. Visualizing While Affirming:

As you repeat your affirmations, take a moment to visualize the reality you are creating. Imagine yourself surrounded by love, feeling the warmth of connection; see yourself growing spiritually, filled with wisdom and peace; picture abundance flowing into your life, bringing joy and opportunities. Engaging your emotions during this process amplifies the effectiveness of your affirmations.

6. Embracing Gratitude:

After reciting your affirmations, take a moment to express gratitude for the love, spiritual insight, and abundance that are already part of your life. Gratitude opens your heart and draws more positive events and outcomes into your life.

CHAPTER 2

Integrating White Witchcraft with Faith

Have you ever found yourself in a place where everything just clicks? Like when you're sipping your morning coffee, the sun is shining just right, and you suddenly understand the meaning of life—or at least the meaning of a good brew. My first experience of integrating white witchcraft with faith was a bit like that. It was an "AHA!" moment that felt like putting the last piece in a jigsaw puzzle. I realized that the boundaries between spiritual paths weren't as rigid as I'd imagined. Instead, they flowed together like a beautiful mosaic, each piece enhancing the other. This revelation opened a world where faith and magic danced together, creating something truly extraordinary.

2.1 THE INTERSECTION OF JUDAISM AND WHITE WITCHCRAFT

When you think about Judaism and white witchcraft, they might seem like an odd couple at first, much like a cat and a dog sharing a sunny window ledge. But dig a little deeper, and you'll find a treasure trove of shared values. Both traditions hold life and the natural world in high regard. Tikkun Olam, or "repairing the world," is a Jewish concept that resonates beautifully with the witch's call to heal and protect. It's about making the world a better place, one small act at a time. Whether you're lighting candles for Shabbat or casting a spell to mend a broken heart, the intention is the same: to bring light and love into the world. Jews pray to one God, referred to as Yahweh. God is viewed as the creator of the universe, a singular and all-powerful being who is actively involved in the world and in the lives of individuals. Jewish prayer often includes a focus on worship, gratitude, and the seeking of guidance, and it is expressed through various traditional prayers and blessings.

Jewish symbols can add a meaningful layer to your rituals, connecting you to a rich tapestry of history and spirituality. Consider incorporating a Star of David or a menorah in your ritual setup, each representing a facet of Jewish heritage. These symbols can serve as focal points for meditation or as part of a ritual aimed at healing and protection. Imagine a quiet evening where you light a menorah not just for its traditional significance, but to invoke a sense of peace and connection in your magical work. This blending of symbols creates a bridge between the two practices, enriching your spiritual experience and grounding your intentions in a profound shared heritage.

Prayer holds a special place in both Judaism and witchcraft, acting as a conduit for intention and divine connection. In Jewish tradition, prayers are whispered, chanted, or sung, each word carrying the weight of centuries of faith. In your magical practice, you can create prayers that align with your intentions, calling for protection and healing. Picture yourself, candles flickering nearby, as you whisper words of power and hope, each syllable a step closer to your heart's desire. These prayers become spells in their own right, woven with the threads of your faith and the magic of your intentions. It's a seamless integration, like a perfectly brewed cup of tea warming you from the inside out.

Jewish holidays offer a rich backdrop for magical rituals, each celebration steeped in tradition and meaning. Take Shabbat, for example—a time for rest and reflection. It's an ideal moment to pause, light candles, and set intentions for the coming week. You might find yourself weaving a spell for clarity or peace, drawing on the quiet energy of Shabbat to focus your magic to bring further love, peace and positive outcomes into your life. Then there's Sukkot, the festival celebrating the harvest. Envision a ritual where you gather with friends, sharing food and gratitude, each bite a celebration of abundance and community. These holidays provide a natural framework for magic, infusing your rituals with depth and further developing your loving relationships with family and friends.

For those intrigued by the mystical, elements of Kabbalah offer a rich vein to tap into. This ancient Jewish mysticism explores the nature of the universe and our place within it, much like the magical practices we embrace. The Tree of Life, the central symbol in Kabbalah, can guide your spiritual growth, offering insights into the interconnectedness of all things. Picture it as a map, each branch a pathway to understanding and enlightenment. In your magical practice, you might meditate on the Tree of Life, visualizing its branches extending into your own life, nurturing your growth and guiding your journey. This exploration of Hebrew mysticism enriches your practice, adding layers of meaning and connection for your life and a sense of well-being that will continue to grow.

Reflection Exercise: Finding Your Spiritual Blend

- Who: Yourself
- What: A reflective journaling exercise to explore your spiritual connections
- Where: A quiet, comfortable space
- When: Anytime you feel the need to deepen your spiritual understanding
- Why: To integrate your faith and magical practice in a meaningful way

1. Begin by reflecting on the values and beliefs that resonate with you in both Judaism and witchcraft.
2. Write down any symbols, holidays, or prayers that hold special meaning for you in each tradition.
3. Consider how these elements can be woven into your magical practice. Do they inspire any specific rituals or intentions?
4. Reflect on how these integrated practices make you feel. Do they bring you a sense of peace, empowerment, or connection?
5. Conclude with a few sentences about what you've discovered and how you might incorporate these insights into your daily life.

By exploring these intersections, you open yourself to a world where faith and magic become partners, each enhancing and enriching the other. As you continue to blend your spiritual paths, you'll find new ways to connect with the divine and deepen your magical practice.

2.2 CHRISTIANITY AND THE WHITE WITCH'S PATH

Christians primarily pray to God, the creator and sustainer of the universe. In Christianity, God is often understood as a Trinity, consisting of God the Father, God the Son, Jesus Christ, and God the Holy Spirit. Christians also pray to Jesus, as the mediator between God and humanity, and some traditions encourage prayers to saints or the Virgin Mary for intercession. Stepping into the world of Christianity and white witchcraft might feel like trying to blend two different flavors into a new dish. You might wonder if they can coexist without clashing. But imagine a sweet and savory combination that surprises you with its harmony. At the core of both, you find an emphasis on love, forgiveness, and kindness. Christian tenets like agape love—unconditional, selfless love—are not just ideals in the church pews but are alive and well in magical practices too. Agape love becomes a guiding star in your magical work, infusing your intentions with compassion and sincerity. When you cast a spell for healing or peace, it's this love that amplifies your intentions, making them resonate far beyond your immediate circle. It's like sending a heartfelt letter that reaches its recipient with just the right words.

Forgiveness is another shared theme that holds power in both Christianity and witchcraft. In the Christian tradition, forgiveness is the key to releasing negativity and finding peace. It's like letting go of a heavy burden, freeing yourself to embrace new possibilities. In your magical practice, you can create forgiveness rituals that mirror this transformative process. Imagine lighting a candle, symbolizing a fresh start, as you focus on letting go of past grievances. You might write down what you wish to release on a piece of paper and then throw it away. This ritual not only clears your emotional slate but also energizes your spellwork, opening pathways for new growth and happiness.

The Bible, with its rich tapestry of verses, offers a myriad of affirmations and mantras for your rituals. These texts have been recited and revered for centuries, carrying a unique power and resonance. Psalms, for example, are often used for peace and protection, their poetic lines creating a shield around you as you work your magic. Proverbs, with their nuggets of wisdom, can guide you in moments of uncertainty, offering clarity and insight. Picture yourself in a quiet space, a Bible open before you, as you select verses that speak to your heart. You can incorporate these into your rituals, chanting them softly as you light a candle or focus your intentions. This practice grounds your magic in tradition and infuses it with a sense of timeless wisdom.

Christian symbols can also enhance your witchcraft practices, adding layers of meaning and protection. The cross, for instance, is more than a symbol of faith; it's a powerful emblem of protection. You might wear a cross as an amulet or place one in your quiet space, inviting its protective energy. Candles, another staple of both Christian and magical rituals, can serve as beacons of hope and intention. Imagine lighting a candle in a dim room, its flickering light casting shadows and shapes, as you offer a prayer or set your intentions. The warmth and glow create a sacred atmosphere, connecting you with the divine and anchoring your magical work.

Community, a cornerstone of Christianity, also plays a vital role in witchcraft. Both paths emphasize the importance of connection and support, recognizing that we are stronger when we stand together. Group prayers and communal rituals offer a sense of belonging and shared purpose. You might join a circle of fellow practitioners, each bringing their energy and intentions to a shared ritual that you agree serves each other and the higher good of humanity. As you hold hands or stand in a circle, you feel the collective power of community, each person contributing to a greater whole. These gatherings not only strengthen your magical practice but also provide a network of support, a reminder that you are never alone on your path.

Building support networks is another way to nurture your practice within a community. Whether it's a formal group like a coven or an informal group of like-minded individuals, these networks offer guidance, encouragement, and friendship. You might organize regular meetings, where you share experiences, learn from one another, and plan communal rituals. In these spaces, you find the freedom to explore your magic, knowing you are supported and accepted. It's like having a safety net, there to catch you when you need it, allowing you to soar higher and explore further. Through community, you find the strength to deepen your practice, embracing both your Christian faith and your magical path with open arms.

2.3 EMBRACING BUDDHIST PRINCIPLES IN MAGIC

Buddhists may revere the Buddha (Siddhartha Gautama) as an enlightened teacher and guide, yet most Buddhists do not focus on the worship of a singular God in the same way many other religions do. They practice meditation and follow the teachings of the Buddha, which emphasize personal spiritual development, ethical conduct, and understanding the nature of reality. In some traditions, there may also be reverence for bodhisattvas or other enlightened beings who assist others on their spiritual paths. So, if you were to sit cross-legged on a cushion, eyes closed, breathing in the peace of the moment you may be on your path to enlightenment. This is the heart of Buddhist mindfulness, a practice that invites you to be fully present, aware, and connected to the now. Mindfulness is a magical tool in its own right, enhancing your spellwork by sharpening focus and intention. Picture yourself about to cast a spell: instead of rushing in, you pause, taking deep, mindful breaths. Each inhale draws in clarity, while each exhale releases distractions. This simple exercise centers you, ensuring that your magical intentions are as clear as a mountain stream. Mindfulness transforms your spellcasting into a dance of awareness, each move deliberate and infused with presence.

Buddhism offers a form of wisdom that aligns beautifully with magical practice. Take the Four Noble Truths, for instance. These truths guide you in understanding desire and suffering, offering insights that can shape ethical and intentional magic. You begin by identifying your desires, not as cravings, but as intentions that can guide your spells. What do you truly seek? Is it love, peace, or perhaps the strength to face life's challenges? By setting clear intentions, you align your magic with your deepest values, ensuring that each spell is a reflection of your authentic self. This process is like tuning an instrument, each note harmonizing with your inner truth, creating a symphony of magical intention.

The Eightfold Path is another gem from Buddhist tradition that can enrich your witchcraft practices. This path, with its emphasis on right intention and right mindfulness, provides a framework for living and practicing magic with integrity. When creating spells, you start with the right intention, ensuring your goals are in harmony with your values and the greater good. It's like planting a seed in fertile soil, nurturing it with care and compassion. Daily rituals then become opportunities to practice right mindfulness, infusing each moment with awareness and intention. Imagine beginning your day with a simple ritual, perhaps lighting a candle and setting an intention for mindfulness. This practice grounds you, aligning your actions and thoughts with your magical and spiritual goals.

Buddhist concepts of impermanence also play a vital role in magic, encouraging you to embrace change and transformation. In a world where nothing stays the same, magic becomes a tool for navigating life's ebb and flow. Rituals for embracing change help you adapt and thrive, turning challenges into opportunities for growth. Picture a ritual where you release old patterns, letting go of what no longer serves you. Perhaps you write down limiting beliefs on paper and then throw it away. This act of letting go is both symbolic and transformative, clearing the way for new possibilities. It's like opening the windows of your soul, allowing fresh air to sweep through and rejuvenate your spirit.

Embracing impermanence also means learning to let go of attachment in your intentions. In magic, as in life, holding on too tightly can stifle growth and creativity. By releasing attachment, you allow your intentions to flow freely, trusting the universe to bring about the best possible outcome. Imagine casting a spell with an open heart, setting your intention and then letting it go, like releasing a balloon into the sky. You watch it rise, confident that it will find its way to where it needs to be. This practice of non-attachment frees you from the weight of expectation, allowing your magic to unfold naturally and beautifully.

As you integrate Buddhist principles into your magical practice, you discover a path that is both grounded and expansive. Mindfulness, intention, and acceptance of change become your allies, guiding you in creating a life filled with purpose and magic. Each breath, each intention, and each spell becomes an opportunity to connect with your inner self and the world around you. It's a path of discovery and transformation, where magic and mindfulness walk hand in hand.

2.4 HINDUISM'S INFLUENCE ON WHITE MAGIC PRACTICES

Hinduism is a polytheistic religion in which each major god, such as Brahma, the creator, Vishnu, the preserver, and Shiva, the destroyer, among others represent different aspects of the divine and have their own unique attributes and stories. Additionally, many Hindus may also worship goddesses such as Saraswati, Lakshmi, and Durga, reflecting the belief in the feminine divine. Digging deeper into the rich spiritual landscape of Hinduism and its influence on white magic is like stepping into a vibrant tapestry of colors, sounds, and scent. Hindu deities, each with their own unique attributes, can inspire and enhance your magical practice. Take Ganesha, for example, known as the remover of obstacles. Invoking Ganesha in your rituals can help clear the path ahead, whether you're embarking on a new project or seeking clarity in your personal life. Picture lighting a candle in his honor, the flame flickering with the promise of new beginnings and the dissolution of barriers. Lakshmi, the goddess of prosperity, offers another layer of depth to your practice. Her presence invites abundance and good fortune. When you create a prosperity spell, consider including symbols or offerings that honor Lakshmi, like a small dish of coins or a fragrant flower. As you focus your intention, envision her blessings pouring into your life, filling it with richness and fulfillment.

The power of mantras and chants in Hinduism is like a secret spice in your magical recipe, enhancing focus and intention. The simple yet profound sound of "Om" is a universal connection, resonating through your being like a gentle bell. As you chant "Om," feel its vibrations align your energy with the universe, creating a sense of peace and unity. Mantras for inner peace, such as "Shanti," can be woven into your rituals, calming your mind and centering your spirit. Picture a quiet moment where you sit cross-legged, eyes closed, repeating a mantra softly to yourself. Each repetition is like a pebble dropped into a still pond, creating ripples of tranquility that spread through your consciousness. These chants become an anchor, grounding your magic in the ancient wisdom of sound and vibration.

Hindu festivals offer a wealth of inspiration for enriching your magical rituals. Diwali, the festival of lights, symbolizes the triumph of light over darkness and is a perfect time for new beginnings. Imagine crafting a ritual where you light small lamps or candles, each one representing a fresh start or a new intention. As the lights flicker, visualize them illuminating your path, banishing shadows, and inviting clarity into your life. Holi, the festival of colors, celebrates transformation and renewal. Picture a gathering where you and loved ones toss colored powders into the air, each splash of color a symbol of the joy and potential for change. As you participate in these vibrant celebrations, you invite their energy into your magical practice, aligning your rituals with the cycles of celebration and renewal.

The concept of dharma in Hinduism provides a guiding principle for your ethical witchcraft practices. Dharma refers to your life purpose and duty, the path that aligns with your true self and the greater good. In your magical work, aligning with dharma means crafting rituals that reflect your values and responsibilities. Imagine a ritual where you seek guidance in discovering your life purpose, perhaps through meditation or divination. As you connect with your inner wisdom, you gain clarity on the actions and decisions that align with your dharma. Aligning your actions with spiritual duties is like tuning an instrument, each note resonating in harmony with the universe. As you honor your dharma, your magic becomes a reflection of your true self, a practice that supports your growth and contributes to the world.

Incorporating these elements of Hinduism into your white magic practice opens a gateway to deeper understanding and connection to yourself and to the manifestations you have both spiritually and physically. The deities, mantras, festivals, and concepts of dharma enhance your rituals, infusing them with ancient wisdom and vibrant energy. Each practice becomes a thread in the tapestry of your spiritual journey, woven with intention and insight. As you explore these influences, you find new layers of meaning in your magic, each one a step closer to the divine. And with each step, you discover a path that is uniquely yours, a blend of traditions that speaks to your soul and empowers your practice.

2.5 CREATING RITUALS THAT HONOR YOUR FAITH

Blending religious practices with witchcraft is like creating a delicious fusion dish—each element retains its unique flavor, yet together they create something entirely new and delightful. Picture this: you're in your sacred space, surrounded by the comforting symbols of your faith and the tools of your magical practice. It's not about picking one over the other but finding harmony between them. You might personalize rituals by incorporating elements that resonate with your spiritual beliefs. Perhaps it's a prayer from your childhood or a meditation technique you learned at a retreat. Each choice adds layers of depth to your practice, making it a true reflection of your spiritual journey. This personalization turns your rituals into intimate expressions of your beliefs, creating a space where your faith and magic coexist in harmony.

Sacred texts are rich with inspiration, offering guidance and wisdom that can deepen your magical practice. These texts have been revered for centuries, their words echoing through time with a power that can enhance your rituals. You might use these texts to create affirmations, distilling their essence into statements that align with your intentions. Imagine finding a verse that speaks to you, then transforming it into an affirmation that you repeat as you work your magic. It's like taking a sip of your favorite tea, letting its warmth fill you with comfort and clarity. Parables, too, offer insights that can enrich your practice. Reflect on their lessons, considering how they apply to your life and your magical goals. This reflection becomes a dialogue between you and the divine, a conversation that guides your path and shapes your intentions.

Religious observances provide a natural rhythm to life, marking time with celebrations, fasts, and reflections. These observances offer a framework for integrating your faith into your daily magical practice. During fasting periods, for instance, you might focus on rituals that emphasize reflection and renewal. Picture a quiet evening where you light a candle, its flame a reminder of your intentions and commitments. As you meditate or journal, you reflect on what you wish to release and what you hope to invite into your life. These rituals transform observances into opportunities for spiritual growth, aligning your magic with the cycles of your faith.

Rituals serve as bridges to deeper connections with the divine, offering moments of reflection and insight that enhance your spirituality. They invite you to pause, breathe, and engage with the sacred. Consider a simple reflective practice, such as spending a few minutes each day in silent contemplation. During this time, you might focus on a question or intention, letting your thoughts and feelings rise to the surface. This practice becomes a mirror, reflecting your inner landscape and revealing new paths for inner exploration. As you engage with these rituals, you foster a sense of connection and community, both with the divine and with those who share your path.

Fostering spiritual growth and connection is at the heart of integrating faith and witchcraft. It's about nurturing your relationship with the divine, allowing it to guide your practice and enrich your life. Rituals become touchstones, moments where you can pause and reconnect with your spiritual core. They offer solace in times of uncertainty and celebration in times of joy. As you create these rituals, you build a practice that is uniquely yours, one that honors your beliefs and supports your growth. This integration becomes a dance, a fluid movement between faith and magic that enhances both.

This chapter has explored the beautiful intersections between faith and white witchcraft, offering pathways for integration and growth. As you continue your exploration, remember that this journey is personal and unique. There's no right or wrong way to blend these practices—only the way that feels authentic to you. This exploration leads us into the next chapter, where we will delve deeper into the tools and techniques that support your magical practice.

CHAPTER 3

Building a Supportive Magical Community

I magine you're at a party, the kind where you don't know anyone, and you're nervously clutching a plate of hors d'oeuvres, wondering if you'll ever find someone who shares your love for both ancient rituals and modern memes. Finding like-minded individuals in your community can feel a bit like that at first. But fear not, fellow seeker of the arcane! There are plenty of places where you can meet people who are as excited about faith, crystals and cauldrons as you are. It's all about putting yourself out there and embracing the magic of community.

3.1 FINDING LIKE-MINDED INDIVIDUALS

The quest for finding your tribe begins with identifying common interests. Start by attending local spiritual or metaphysical fairs. These events can be an introduction to a vast array of mystical knowledge and potential friendships. As you wander through booths filled with tarot decks and incense, strike up conversations with vendors and fellow attendees. Ask about their practices and share your own experiences. You never know, you might leave with a new friend—and maybe a few crystals you didn't know you needed. Workshops and classes on witchcraft are another great way to meet people who share your passion. Whether it's a class on herbalism or a workshop on moon rituals, these gatherings are perfect for connecting with others eager to learn and share their magical journeys.

Local opportunities abound if you know where to look. Holistic health food stores and restaurants often have community boards brimming with flyers and notices about upcoming events. These boards are like the magical classifieds, offering everything from meditation circles to full-moon gatherings. Keep an eye out for events that pique your interest, and don't be shy about showing up solo—you might just meet your new soulmate. Community events celebrating seasonal changes are another fantastic opportunity to connect. Whether it's a summer solstice festival or an autumn equinox celebration, these events bring together people who appreciate the cycles of nature and the magic they hold. Join in the festivities, and soon you'll find yourself surrounded by kindred spirits who share your love for mystical celebrations.

Networking is a skill that's as crucial in the magical world as it is in the mundane. Think of it as casting a net wide to catch as many potential connections as possible. When you attend events, initiate conversations with those around you. It can be as simple as complimenting someone's book selection or asking about their favorite magical practice. Don't be afraid to offer your skills or knowledge in exchange for collaboration. Maybe you're great at crafting herbal sachets, or you have a knack for reading tarot. Sharing your talents not only helps others but also opens doors to new connections and friendships.

Sometimes, though, local options might be scarce, and it can feel like you're the only witch in your neck of the woods. Fear not! You have the power to create your own opportunities for connection. Consider hosting a meetup in a local park. It doesn't have to be fancy; just a gathering of like-minded individuals sharing stories, ideas, and maybe a few magical tips. Or organize a book club focused on witchcraft literature. Choose a book, invite some friends, and let the discussions flow. These gatherings can be as formal or informal as you like, and they provide a wonderful way to connect with others who share your interests.

Exercise: Crafting Your Community Connection Plan

To help you navigate the world of witchy networking, here's a little exercise to get you started. Grab a notebook or open a new document and jot down some ideas.

1. List Your Interests: Identify specific areas of witchcraft you're passionate about. Is it herbalism, divination, or perhaps lunar magic?
2. Research Local Events: Look up upcoming fairs, workshops, and classes in your area. Note the ones that align with your interests.
3. Set Goals: Decide how many events you'd like to attend each month and what you hope to gain from each experience, whether it's knowledge, connections, or just a good time.
4. Plan Your Approach: Think about how you'll introduce yourself and what you'd like to share about your practice. Practice a few conversation starters if you're feeling nervous.
5. Reflect and Adjust: After attending an event, reflect on your experience. What went well? What could you do differently next time? Use these insights to refine your approach and enhance your community-building efforts.

Building a supportive witchcraft community is like weaving a tapestry of friendships and connections. It takes time, patience, and a bit of courage, but the rewards are well worth the effort. You'll find yourself surrounded by people who understand your quirks, share your passions, and support your magical journey.

3.2 ONLINE PLATFORMS FOR COMMUNITY ENGAGEMENT

In today's tech-savvy world, finding a community can be as easy as opening your laptop. Online platforms offer dozens of options to make connections, each waiting to be discovered. Witchcraft-focused Facebook groups are one such goldmine. These groups range from the broad and bustling to the niche and cozy, offering a place for every kind of practitioner. You may find ways to begin scrolling through posts filled with tips on spells, discussions on ritual techniques, and supportive comments that feel like a virtual hug. Whether you're a solitary witch seeking insights or someone eager to share your own experiences, these groups offer a welcoming digital hearth. Then there are forums like Reddit, where specialized witchcraft websites provide endless threads rich with knowledge. Here, you can dive into discussions on everything from the historical roots of certain practices to the latest trends in crystal use. These spaces are like the bustling marketplaces of the ancient world, filled with voices eager to share, learn, and grow.

But as with any community, online or offline, etiquette plays a crucial role. Think of it as the unwritten rule book that keeps interactions respectful and enjoyable. First and foremost, set boundaries for personal information sharing. It's all too easy to get caught up in the excitement and share more than you intend. Remember that while the digital world connects us, it also requires a level of caution. Protect your privacy and respect the privacy of others. Equally important is respecting differing opinions and practices. The beauty of online platforms lies in their diversity, with members bringing a multitude of perspectives to the table. Approach each discussion with an open mind, ready to learn from those who may see the world a bit differently. Engaging in respectful dialogue not only enriches your understanding but also fosters a community where all feel valued and heard.

Active participation is the magic ingredient that turns an online platform from a mere website into a thriving community. Dive into discussions and share your experiences, whether you're recounting a successful spell or pondering a question that's been on your mind. Remember, your voice adds value to the conversation. Offer support and advice to others, drawing from your own journey and knowledge. Maybe someone's seeking guidance on using herbs in their practice, and you happen to have just the recipe for a soothing herbal sachet. Sharing these insights doesn't just help others; it also strengthens your own connection to the community. Picture it as a lively roundtable, each participant contributing their unique perspective, creating a tapestry of shared wisdom and support.

Digital tools can transform online interactions into something truly special. Video conferencing platforms, for instance, offer the chance to participate in virtual rituals. Imagine joining a circle of practitioners from around the globe, each one lighting a candle in their own space, their faces illuminated by the soft glow of a shared ritual. It's a powerful reminder that magic knows no borders. Shared documents can also facilitate collaborative projects, whether you're working on a group spell or compiling a resource list for new practitioners. These tools help bridge the gap between the digital and the personal, allowing for a deeper level of engagement and connection. The possibilities are as limitless as your imagination, offering new ways to build and nurture your community.

Online platforms are a vibrant tapestry of possibilities, offering connections that stretch across continents and cultures. They're a modern meeting place, where seekers of all varieties can gather to share insights, support one another, and grow together. The digital world may seem vast and impersonal at first glance, but within it lies the potential for deep and meaningful connections. As you explore these platforms, remember that each interaction is an opportunity: to learn, to teach, and to form bonds that transcend the boundaries of time and space. So go ahead, dive into the world of online witchcraft communities, and discover the wealth of knowledge and camaraderie that awaits.

3.3 HOSTING OR JOINING WITCHCRAFT CIRCLES

Imagine standing in a circle of fellow seekers, each person holding a candle, their faces lit by the warm glow of shared intention. That's the magic of a witchcraft circle. These gatherings amplify energy, turning individual sparks into a blazing bonfire of collective power. Picture it as a potluck for the soul, where everyone brings their unique strengths, perspectives, and techniques to the table. You get to learn from others, share your own insights, and together, create something greater than the sum of its parts. Circles are not just about casting spells; they're about weaving a tapestry of community spirit, one thread at a time.

If you decide to host your own circle, there are a few steps that can help ensure its success. First, find a location that feels both sacred and welcoming. It could be a cozy living room, a sunny backyard, or even a local park. Just make sure it's a space where everyone can feel comfortable and safe. Timing is also crucial. Choose a time that works for most members, and consider aligning it with lunar phases or seasonal celebrations for that extra touch of magic. Once you've got the logistics down, focus on creating an inclusive atmosphere. Greet each member warmly, encourage introductions, and set the tone with a brief opening ritual that invites everyone to relax and open up. Think of it as setting the stage for a magical play, where everyone knows their lines and feels part of the performance.

Joining a circle, on the other hand, can be just as rewarding. It's a chance to build deep, lasting connections with people who understand your quirks and passions. Picture it as finding your tribe, a group of kindred spirits who support and celebrate you and vice versa. In these gatherings, you gain confidence through shared experiences, learning from others while contributing your own knowledge. Everyone's a teacher, and everyone's a student. The bonds you form can last a lifetime, offering support and friendship through the ups and downs of your spiritual path. It's like having a safety net woven from the threads of trust, understanding, and shared magic.

The activities you engage in during circle meetings can be as varied as the members themselves. Group meditations are a beautiful way to start, each breath synchronizing with the next, creating a wave of calm and focus. Intention-setting rituals follow naturally, allowing everyone to voice their hopes and desires, infusing the circle with purpose and direction. Collaborative spellwork is where the real fun begins. Imagine crafting a spell together, each member contributing their unique energy and expertise. Perhaps it's a spell for healing, prosperity, or protection, with everyone focusing their intentions on a common goal. Seasonal celebrations add another layer of richness, marking the passage of time and the cycles of nature. Whether it's a solstice feast or an equinox ceremony, these celebrations connect you to the earth and its rhythms, grounding your practice in the ancient dance of the seasons.

Rituals and activities in a circle are not just about the magic; they're about the connections forged in the process. They offer a chance to learn from diverse perspectives, each member bringing a different flavor to the mix. You might discover a new technique for casting a circle or learn about a herb you'd never considered using. These gatherings are fertile ground for creativity and growth, a place where you can explore new ideas and refine your practice. Whether you're hosting or joining, circles offer a space to connect, learn, and create magic together, turning the ordinary into the extraordinary with every meeting.

3.4 SHARING EXPERIENCES AND LEARNING TOGETHER

There's something magical about sharing experiences and knowledge within a community, akin to gathering around a campfire where stories are exchanged and connections are forged. In the world of witchcraft, this shared learning is invaluable. Imagine your group sitting together, each bringing their unique tales and insights to the table. One might share the story of a spell that went delightfully sideways, leading to unexpected but welcome results. Another might offer insights gleaned from years of practice, providing wisdom that could only come from firsthand experience. This exchange isn't just about information; it's about creating bonds and building a web of collective wisdom that benefits everyone involved. By pooling our experiences, we engage in collective problem-solving, turning challenges into opportunities for creativity and growth.

Facilitating open communication is crucial for this kind of shared learning to thrive. It's about creating spaces where people feel safe to voice their thoughts and challenges without fear of judgment. Regular discussion sessions can help foster this environment. Picture a cozy setting where everyone feels comfortable enough to share their trials and triumphs, knowing that they're among friends who understand and support them. It's like having a soft landing spot for your worries and a springboard for your ideas. Creating these safe spaces might involve setting some ground rules, like ensuring everyone gets a chance to speak or agreeing to keep personal stories confidential. These guidelines help maintain an atmosphere of trust and respect, encouraging honest and open dialogue.

Collaborative learning also plays a pivotal role in community building. By organizing skill-sharing workshops, we can tap into the diverse talents and knowledge that each member brings. Imagine a weekend workshop where one person teaches the art of crafting herbal sachets while another leads a session on tarot reading. It's like a magical swap meet, with each participant walking away with new skills and insights. Group book study sessions on witchcraft topics are another way to engage in collaborative learning. Choose a book, dive into its pages together, and then gather to discuss its themes and ideas. These sessions are not just about understanding the material but also about seeing how it applies to our own practices and lives. Each discussion is an opportunity to learn from different perspectives, broadening our understanding of the craft.

Celebrating collective achievements is the paragon of community engagement. Acknowledging successes, whether big or small, not only boosts morale but also strengthens the bonds within the group. Hosting seasonal festivals or ceremonies can be a wonderful way to mark these milestones. Imagine a gathering where everyone comes together to celebrate the turning of the seasons, each person's contributions recognized and appreciated. It's like throwing a party where everyone gets to be the guest of honor. Creating awards or recognitions for contributions is another way to celebrate achievements. Whether it's a simple certificate of appreciation or a token that symbolizes the recipient's impact, these acknowledgments remind us that our efforts are valued and that we're all part of something larger than ourselves.

Sharing experiences and learning together transforms a group of individuals into a cohesive community. It's about lifting each other up, learning from one another, and celebrating the journey we share. Each interaction, each story told, and each bit of wisdom shared adds to the richness of the community, making it a place of growth, support, and joy.

3.5 FOSTERING A POSITIVE AND INCLUSIVE ENVIRONMENT

Creating a supportive and inclusive environment is like crafting the perfect potion—it requires the right mix of ingredients, a dash of care, and a sprinkle of intention. Inclusivity is the secret ingredient that ensures everyone feels welcome, regardless of their background or experience level. One way to cultivate this is by establishing a code of conduct for interactions. Think of it as the unspoken rules of engagement, ensuring respect and kindness permeate every interaction. Encourage diverse participation and representation, because let's be honest—variety is the spice of life. By inviting voices from different walks of life, you enrich the community tapestry, weaving together a colorful array of perspectives and experiences.

Addressing conflict is inevitable in any community, much like an unexpected rain shower at a picnic. But fear not! With the right strategies, you can turn potential storms into gentle drizzles. Mediation techniques are invaluable tools for resolving disputes. They involve listening, understanding, and finding common ground, like a peaceful clearing in a forest. Setting clear communication expectations helps prevent misunderstandings before they start. Encourage members to express their thoughts openly, yet respectfully, fostering an environment where everyone feels heard and valued. It's about nurturing a culture where differences are embraced, and conflicts are seen as opportunities for growth rather than hurdles.

Encouraging personal growth within the community is akin to tending a garden. Each member is a unique plant with their own needs, strengths, and potential. Mentorship programs can be the sunlight that helps these plants flourish. Pairing experienced members with newcomers fosters a sense of belonging and accelerates learning. It's a two-way street, where both mentor and mentee gain fresh insights and perspectives. Encourage goal setting and accountability partnerships. These partnerships act as the gardener's gentle hand, guiding each member toward their aspirations while offering support and encouragement. It's about creating a space where growth is celebrated, and members feel empowered to reach their full potential.

Sustaining community engagement is like keeping a fire burning bright. It requires regular tending, a bit of creativity, and a willingness to experiment with new ideas. Regularly rotating leadership roles can inject fresh energy into the group, preventing stagnation and encouraging diverse voices to lead, which is like passing the baton in a relay race, ensuring everyone has a chance to shine. Hosting themed events or challenges is another fantastic way to maintain ubiquitous interest. Imagine a monthly challenge where members explore different aspects of witchcraft, from crafting talismans to studying ancient texts. These activities not only engage members but also foster a sense of camaraderie and shared purpose.

In nurturing a positive and inclusive environment, you create a community that's not just a gathering of individuals but a vibrant, dynamic organism. It's a place where everyone's contribution is valued, where growth is nurtured, and where conflicts are seen as stepping stones to deeper understanding. By fostering such an environment, you lay the groundwork for a community that's resilient, compassionate, and ever-evolving. And as you journey together, you'll find that the bonds you forge are as strong and enduring as the magic you create.

As we wrap up this chapter, remember that building a community is about more than just gathering people; it's about creating a space where everyone feels welcome, heard, and valued. This sense of belonging and support is what turns a group into a true community. In the next chapter, we'll explore the challenges of integrating witchcraft into daily life and how to overcome them with grace and resilience.

CHAPTER 4

Tools and Elements of White Witchcraft

P icture this: you're walking through a sun-drenched meadow, the air filled with the scent of wildflowers, the soft hum of bees and fluttering butterflies. This idyllic scene isn't just the stuff of daydreams; it's the birthplace of herbal magic. Herbs have been used for centuries, their powers harnessed by wise men and women who understood the subtle dance of nature's remedies. Today, you and I can tap into this ancient wisdom, transforming our lives with the simple yet profound magic of herbs. They're more than just garnish for your dinner plate; they're potent allies in your magical toolkit, ready to bring healing and harmony into your life.

Herbs have been the backbone of countless rituals throughout history. Our ancestors knew what they were doing when they reached for a sprig of sage or a handful of lavender. These plants carry the essence of the earth, each with its unique properties and powers. When you incorporate herbs into your practice, you invite the natural world into your circle, fostering a deeper connection with the earth's rhythms. But here's the twist: it's not just about grabbing any old plant and hoping for the best.

Intention is your secret ingredient. When you select herbs with purpose, you magnify their magical potential, transforming a simple ritual into a powerful act of creation.

Let's chat about some of the star players in the herbal world. Lavender, with its calming scent, is your go-to for peace and relaxation. Imagine a stressful day melting away as you bask in the soothing aroma of lavender, feeling your worries drift off like clouds. Rosemary is the guardian of protection and clarity, its sharp scent cutting through confusion like a trusty sword. Picture a rosemary-infused bath after a long day, the steam rising around you as you regain focus and strength. Then there's chamomile, the gentle giant of the herbal world, offering comfort and calm at the end of a hectic day. A cup of chamomile tea can be like a hug in a mug, wrapping you in tranquility and easing you into a restful night's sleep.

Sourcing your herbs ethically is as important as choosing the right ones. Growing your own is a delightful way to ensure you know exactly where your herbs come from. There's nothing quite like the satisfaction of snipping fresh basil from your windowsill garden or harvesting lavender from your backyard. If gardening isn't your thing, no worries! Look for local farmers' markets or trusted suppliers who prioritize sustainable practices. Once you have your herbs, preparation is key. Drying them carefully and storing them in airtight containers keeps their magic potent and ready to be unleashed whenever you need it.

Incorporating herbs into your daily practice can be as simple or as elaborate as you like. Start your day with an herbal tea brewed with intention, each sip a step toward your goals. Whether it's a cup of peppermint for alertness or chamomile for calm, let the herbs guide your day. You can also create herbal sachets, little bundles of magic that tuck neatly under your pillow or in your bag. Think of them as portable spells, infusing your life with their unique energies wherever you go. Whether you're looking for protection, love, or a dash of good luck, there's an herb for that.

Herbal Magic Exercise: Create Your Own Herbal Sachet

- Who: Yourself
- What: A simple exercise to create a personal herbal sachet
- Where: Your sacred space or a quiet corner
- When: Anytime you feel the need for a boost of herbal magic
- Why: To carry the energy of your chosen herbs with you throughout the day

Instructions:

1. Choose your herbs based on your intention—lavender for calm, rosemary for protection, or chamomile for comfort.
2. Gather a small piece of fabric or a muslin bag and some thread. The fabric or bag must be loosely woven.
3. Place the herbs in the center of the fabric, focusing on your intention as you work.
4. Tie the fabric securely to create a sachet.
5. Hold the sachet in your hands, infusing it with your energy and intention.
6. Carry it with you, letting its magic support you throughout the day.

Herbs are a bridge between you and the natural world, a reminder of the magic that surrounds us every day. By inviting them into your practice, you open yourself to their wisdom and power, creating a life filled with wonder and possibility.

4.2 THE POWER OF CRYSTALS IN YOUR PRACTICE

Crystals are like the rock stars of the magical world. They've got this undeniable presence, a kind of energy that makes you stop and take notice. Each crystal pulses with its own unique vibration, just waiting to partner with your intentions to create some serious magic. Let's start with amethyst. It's the go-to crystal for anyone looking to boost their spiritual growth. Its deep purple hue isn't just pretty to look at; it's like a velvety invitation to dive deeper into your spiritual self. When you meditate with amethyst, you might find your mind opening up, ready to absorb the mysteries of the universe. Then there's clear quartz, the workhorse of the crystal world. It's like a megaphone for your intentions, amplifying whatever you're putting out there. If you're feeling a bit stuck or your energy's a bit low, clear quartz is there to give you a gentle nudge, boosting your vibe and helping you shine a little brighter.

Choosing the right crystal can feel like picking a new best friend. You want one that gets you, one that vibes with your energy and intentions. Intuitive selection is key here. Sometimes, it's as simple as letting your gut guide you. Walk into a crystal shop—or scroll through an online one—and see which stones catch your eye. Maybe one feels warm in your hand, or its color just speaks to you. Listen to those subtle cues. They're like little winks from the universe, guiding you to the crystal that's right for you. If you're not sure where to start, think about what you need. Is it clarity, protection, or maybe a little extra love? Match your needs to the properties of the crystals. Each one has its own strengths, so choose the one that aligns with your intentions and watch the magic unfold.

Once you've got your crystal, you want to make sure it's in tip-top shape for your magical work. Crystal care is like giving your stone a little spa day. Cleansing is the first step. Crystals can pick up a lot of energy, so you'll want to clear them of any lingering vibes. Moonlight charging is my favorite method. Just leave your crystal under the light of a full moon, and let it soak up those lunar rays. It's like a day at the spa, leaving your crystal refreshed and ready to go. Programming your crystal comes next. Hold your stone, focus on your intention, and let your energy flow into it. Speak to it, if you like. Tell it what you hope to achieve together. This step personalizes your crystal, making it a true partner in your magical practices.

Integrating crystals into your rituals and spells is where the fun begins. Crystal grids are a powerful way to manifest your desires. Picture a geometric pattern, each point adorned with a crystal, all working together to create a focused energy field. It's like a symphony of stones, each one playing its part to bring your intention to life. If you're looking for a simpler approach, consider carrying a pocket stone. These little gems are like portable protection, keeping you grounded and energized throughout the day. Whether it's a piece of black tourmaline for warding off negativity or a rose quartz for attracting love, having one tucked into your pocket or purse can be a comforting companion as you navigate the world. Crystals, with their ancient wisdom and potent energy, are invaluable allies in your magical practice. Their presence can transform ordinary moments into extraordinary ones, offering guidance, protection, and a touch of sparkle to your everyday life.

4.3 INCORPORATING NATURE INTO YOUR RITUALS

Imagine standing barefoot on cool grass, the sun warming your skin while a gentle breeze whispers through the trees. This connection with nature isn't just a feel-good moment; it's a core part of white witchcraft. Nature is the original source of magic, offering its bounty to those who seek to align with its rhythms.

Grounding exercises in natural settings can help you tap into this energy. Picture yourself seated under a tree, roots stretching deep into the earth. As you breathe, visualize those roots drawing up strength and stability, grounding you as you prepare for your magical work. This connection isn't just about borrowing nature's power; it's about recognizing that you're a part of this vast, interconnected web of life.

Seasonal rituals aligned with the earth's cycles are another way to honor this connection. These rituals aren't just about marking time; they're about tuning in to the earth's energy and letting it guide your practice. During the spring, when life awakens and blossoms, consider rituals that focus on new beginnings and growth. In the fall, as the world prepares for rest, your rituals might center on gratitude and reflection. Each season brings its unique energy, and by aligning your practices with these cycles, you deepen your connection to the natural world. It's like dancing with the earth, each step in harmony with its eternal rhythm.

Now, let's talk about the elements: water, fire, earth, and air. They're not just building blocks of the physical world; they're vital components of your magical practice. Incorporating these elements into your rituals can enhance their power and meaning. Imagine using rainwater for a cleansing ritual, its natural purity washing away negativity and refreshing your spirit. Picture a feather, light and delicate, representing the air's freedom and inspiration. As you hold it, focus on the ideas and insights you wish to invite into your life. Each element carries its unique energy, and by weaving them into your practice, you create a tapestry of intention and power.

As modern witches, it's essential to embrace eco-friendly practices. Mother Earth is generous, but she needs our care in return. When gathering natural elements, opt for sustainable choices. Harvest fallen leaves and branches instead of cutting live plants. These materials are gifts from the earth, already offered with love. Use biodegradable materials in your rituals, ensuring that your magical work leaves no trace behind. It's about creating a positive alliance with nature, one that respects its beauty and ensures its longevity. This eco-conscious approach not only enhances your magic but also strengthens your bond with the earth.

Outdoor rituals offer a unique opportunity to deepen your connection with nature. There's something profoundly moving about conducting a full moon ceremony in an open space, the moon's soft glow illuminating your circle. As you stand beneath the night sky, you feel the universe's vastness, its mysteries unfolding around you. Engage in nature walks with intention setting, each step a meditation on your goals and desires. Let the rustle of leaves and the songs of birds accompany your thoughts, guiding you to clarity and insight. These outdoor activities aren't just about doing magic; they're about experiencing it, feeling it in your bones as you engage with the world around you.

Incorporating nature into your rituals is a practice that invites you to pause, breathe, and listen. It's about recognizing the world's magic, a magic that's always been there, waiting for you to see it. By aligning your practice with nature, you open yourself to its wisdom and power. You become a part of something greater, a dance of life that stretches beyond time and space. This connection isn't just for your rituals; it's for your soul, a reminder that you are never alone in your magical journey. Nature stands with you, a steadfast ally in your quest for love, happiness, and abundance.

4.4 CRAFTING PERSONAL TALISMANS

Imagine stepping out into the world with a little extra spring in your step, knowing you've got a secret ally tucked away in your pocket or hanging around your neck. That's the magic of talismans. These small, often unassuming objects are imbued with purpose and energy, serving as focal points for your intentions. Think of them as your personal cheerleaders, whispering encouragement and protection as you navigate your day. Talismans can be crafted for various purposes, such as protection during travel or enhancing love in relationships. Picture a protective talisman as a tiny guardian that ensures safe passage and smooth journeys, or a love talisman that gently nudges you toward deeper connections and understanding with those you cherish. These little powerhouses work quietly, yet their impact can be profound, subtly shifting the energies around you to align with your desires.

Creating a talisman is a deeply personal process, one that allows you to pour your intentions into a physical form. Start by selecting materials that resonate with your goal. Each material carries its unique energy, so choose with care. Maybe you're drawn to a smooth river stone or a piece of wood carved with care. Let your intuition guide you, as it often knows what you need before your mind does. Once you've chosen your materials, it's time to infuse them with energy and purpose. Hold the object in your hands and focus on your intention. Visualize your goal as a vivid image, letting the energy flow from your heart into the talisman. This act of imbuing your talisman with intention is like breathing life into it, transforming it from a simple object into a powerful tool.

Symbols and motifs can add a layer of depth and power to your talismans. They act as visual anchors, focusing your mind and intention on the desired outcome. Sigils, for example, are symbols created for specific outcomes, often a combination of letters or shapes that represent your intention. Imagine designing a sigil for success in your career, its curves and lines weaving together to form a unique representation of your goal. Sacred geometry, with its intricate patterns and harmonious structures, can also enhance the power of your talismans. Picture incorporating a simple geometric shape, like a triangle or a circle, to bring balance and focus to your talisman. These symbols are like a secret code, known only to you, that connects your talisman to the energies you wish to harness.

Incorporating talismans into your daily life is both practical and empowering. Wearing them as jewelry keeps their energy close to your body, a constant reminder of your intentions and goals. Imagine slipping on a necklace with a small talisman pendant, its weight a comforting presence throughout your day. Regularly charging your talisman ensures it remains potent and effective. You might choose to place it in the light of the full moon, allowing it to absorb the moon's energy and recharge its power. This ritual not only maintains the talisman's effectiveness but also strengthens your connection to it, making it a living part of your magical practice.

Crafting and using talismans is a journey of discovery and empowerment. These small objects become allies in your magical work, amplifying your intentions and guiding you toward your goals. With each use, your relationship with your talisman deepens, turning it into a trusted companion on your path. As you continue to explore the world of white witchcraft, you'll find that these tools offer both protection and inspiration, enhancing your practice in ways you never imagined. Through talismans, you engage with the magic of intention and creation, crafting a life filled with purpose, love, and abundance.

Share the Secret Sauce of White Witchcraft

"You've always had the power, my dear. You just had to learn it for yourself."

— THE WIZARD OF OZ

Mention the word "witchcraft" to someone unaware of this ancient practice and it may conjure up images of boiling cauldrons, frogs, and potions. Yet, white witchcraft is centered on anything but using power for evil purposes or manipulating outcomes for the worse. Instead, it's all about love... building a haven in your mind and heart so you can bring love, light, and inspiration to others. I hope that even though you're only halfway through the book, you've already begun living with intention, creating rituals that honor your faith, and collecting tools and elements for use in your rituals. As you've seen, an exercise as simple as collecting a desired herb and carrying it with you in a sachet can help set your intention for the day—be it to curb stress, feel more comforted, or enjoy a powerful sense of connection.

The modern-day white witch integrates her goals and faith into her witchcraft. She is positive, purposeful, and goal-oriented. I have shown you how easy it is to combine your practice with your faith since witchcraft has so much in common with the world's major religions. Wisdom, love, peace... the pursuit of these values is something witchcraft shares with all of them. You have also seen how the modern witch is an eco-warrior; one who respects nature and harnesses its potent benefits, incorporating its most powerful herbs into her rituals.

It inspires me to think of the worlds that witchcraft will open up for you. You can create your own talismans, choose crystals that uplift your energy, and be the protector of the natural world our Planet deserves. If you already feel more empowered by the rituals I've shared with you, please let others know how you feel.

By leaving a review of this book on Amazon, you'll let other readers know that white witchcraft isn't something they have to wonder about... they can live it and practice it every day of their lives.

Thanks for lending me a hand. I hope you're excited about what's up ahead—in the second half of the book, you'll discover many more rituals that will keep you on your path to personal growth.

Scan the QR code below

CHAPTER 5

Developing Your Personal Practice

Have you ever set out on a road trip with no map, no GPS, just a vague idea that you wanted to end up somewhere warm and sunny? Setting intentions in your magical practice is kind of like packing that map, or plugging in that GPS, for your journey. Without those intentions, you might find yourself circling the same roundabout, unsure of whether to take the exit marked "New Beginnings" or "Time for a Nap." Clear intentions are your guide, your roadmap, steering you toward the outcomes you desire. They act like the main source of power for your spells, aligning your thoughts and feelings with the universe's energy. When you set clear intentions, you let the universe know exactly what you're aiming for, preventing any accidental detours into the land of undesired outcomes. Specificity is key. You wouldn't just order "food" at a restaurant, would you? You'd be more specific and say, "I'll have the spaghetti, please!" The same goes for intentions. They need to be specific and aligned with your personal values to really hit the mark.

So how do you craft these magical roadmaps, these intentions, with the finesse of a seasoned cartographer? Enter the SMART criteria: Specific, Measurable, Achievable, Relevant, and Time-bound. This approach ensures your intentions aren't just floating in the ether like a lost balloon. Start by being Specific. If you want more peace in your life, what does that look like? Is it a more peaceful home environment or more peace of mind? Measurable means you know when you've reached your destination. Maybe it's a certain number of peaceful evenings at home per week. Achievable? Make sure it's within reach. If you work 80 hours a week, daily peaceful evenings might be a stretch. Relevant …ties your intention to your larger goals and values. And Time-bound gives it a deadline—otherwise, it's just a dream. Crafting intention statements with this formula is like building a sturdy bridge from where you are to where you want to be.

Visualization is the secret sauce that adds flavor to your intentions, turning them from "meh" to "wow." It's like daydreaming with a purpose. Imagine seeing your intention unfold in your mind's eye, playing out like your own personal movie. Guided imagery exercises can help enhance this skill. Picture yourself walking through a forest, each step bringing you closer to your goal. Or use a vision board to manifest your desires. Gather images, words, and symbols that represent your intention and arrange them where you can see them daily. This visual reminder keeps your intention fresh and vibrant, like a favorite song stuck in your head. Again, the more positive, emotional commitment and intention you have when you visualize what you want, the more you will manifest. The road to get there will be shorter and less circuitous as well.

But how do you turn intentions into a daily practice without it feeling like a chore? Simple rituals can weave intention-setting into the fabric of your everyday life. Morning intention-setting meditations are a great way to start. Picture yourself in a quiet space, sipping your coffee as you focus on the day's goals. Let your mind wander over the possibilities, setting your intention with clarity and purpose. Evening reflection circles offer a chance to review and adjust your intentions. Maybe you gather with friends or simply take a moment to reflect solo. Light a candle, close your eyes, and let your thoughts drift over the day's events. What went well? What needs a little tweak? These rituals create a rhythm, a dance of intention and reflection that guides you toward your goals with grace and ease, as mentioned in chapter one.

Visualization Exercise: Crafting Your Vision Board

- Who: Yourself
- What: A creative exercise to visualize your intentions
- Where: A quiet space with a comfortable surface
- When: Anytime you feel inspired to focus your intentions
- Why: To create a tangible reminder of your goals

1. Gather materials: a board or large piece of paper, magazines, scissors, glue, and markers.
2. Reflect on your intentions. What do you want to manifest?
3. Flip through magazines, cutting out images, words, or phrases that resonate with your goals.
4. Arrange and glue these cutouts onto your board, creating a collage that represents your vision.
5. Add personal touches with markers or other decorations.
6. Place your vision board where you'll see it daily, allowing it to inspire and guide your intentions.

Setting intentions is the heart of your magical practice. It's the compass that guides you, the engine that powers your journey. With clear intentions, you harness the universe's energy, aligning it with your own to create a life that reflects your deepest desires.

5.2 DAILY RITUALS FOR LOVE AND ABUNDANCE

Imagine starting your day not with the blare of an alarm clock, but with a gentle whisper of affirmation. These small, daily rituals are like your morning cup of coffee—refreshing and essential for waking up your spirit. Incorporating daily rituals into your life is more than just a routine; it's a steady rhythm that guides you toward growth. Morning affirmations are a powerful way to center yourself in love and gratitude. As you brush your teeth or sip your tea, take a moment to affirm the love that surrounds you and the abundance you wish to invite. It's like giving your heart a little pep talk, setting a positive tone for the day ahead. And as the sun sets, consider lighting an evening candle for abundance. Watch the flame dance as you reflect on the day's blessings and the prosperity you're welcoming. These rituals are gentle reminders that you're not just going through the motions; you're consciously creating a life filled with love and abundance.

Crafting love-focused rituals can transform your self-care routine into a delightful celebration of you. Picture a heart-opening meditation, where you sit quietly, breathing deeply, and visualize love as a warm, glowing light filling your heart. Feel it expand with each breath, enveloping you in a comforting embrace. This is your time to reconnect with yourself, to acknowledge your worth and beauty. Writing a love letter to yourself is another way to shower yourself with affection. Grab a pen and paper, and let the words flow. Tell yourself what you admire, what you forgive, and what you dream of achieving. These letters are little treasures, capturing the essence of self-love that you can revisit whenever you need a boost of confidence or reassurance.

Rituals for abundance invite the universe to open its arms and shower you with its gifts. Gratitude journaling is a simple yet profound practice that shifts your focus from what's lacking to what's plentiful. Each day, jot down three things you're grateful for, no matter how small. Over time, you'll notice a shift, a lightness in your step as you become more aware of the abundance already present in your life. Prosperity bowls are another fun and tactile way to attract abundance. Fill a bowl with coins and herbs like basil or cinnamon, each symbolizing wealth and prosperity. Place it in a prominent spot in your home. As you add to it, visualize the bounty you're attracting, and feel the excitement of possibility bubbling up inside you.

But let's be real: life isn't always as predictable as one would hope. Sometimes, you need to switch things up. Adaptability and creativity are your best friends in the realm of rituals. Tailor them to suit your energy levels and mood. Feeling rushed in the morning? Keep your affirmations short and sweet, a quick mantra whispered as you dash out the door. On days when you have more time, indulge in a longer meditation or a creative activity that lights you up. Incorporate music or art into your rituals, letting the melodies or brushstrokes guide your intentions. A favorite song can become the backdrop to your evening candle ritual, or a sketchpad might capture the essence of your heart-opening meditation.

The beauty of rituals lies in their flexibility. They're not rigid routines you must follow to the letter although your assiduous, daily commitment to, and unwavering belief in the process are catalysts for its effectiveness. They're living, breathing practices that grow and evolve with you. As you weave these rituals into your life, you're not just creating moments of magic—you're crafting a tapestry of love and abundance that supports and uplifts you every day.

5.3 CREATING A 30-DAY MAGIC JOURNAL

Imagine a magic journal as your personal spellbook, a canvas where your thoughts and experiences take shape, guiding you through the peaks and valleys of your white witchcraft practice. Keeping a magic journal adds a layer of reflection and growth to your journey, almost like having a trusted friend who listens without judgment and keeps all your secrets. This isn't your run-of-the-mill diary; it's a place to document rituals, jot down moments of inspiration, and track your personal evolution. The act of writing can be cathartic and enlightening, helping you recognize patterns and insights you might otherwise miss. The process of writing also helps you clarify your thoughts in a way that distills related thoughts and other intentions. By committing your thoughts to paper, you create a tangible record of your magical progress, something you can look back on and say, "Look how far I've come!"

Setting up your magic journal is a bit like decorating your own magical lair. The first step is choosing a format that suits your style. Maybe you're drawn to a sleek leather-bound notebook, or perhaps a simple spiral-bound journal speaks to you. You could even go digital, using apps that allow for creative expression and easy editing. Whatever you choose, it should feel good in your hands, ready to capture your thoughts whenever inspiration strikes. Decorating your journal with personal symbols is where the fun begins. Perhaps you add a crescent moon sticker or draw a sigil on the cover. These touches personalize your journal, making it a reflection of your magical identity. It's your space, after all; let it be as unique and vibrant as you are.

Daily prompts and exercises can transform your journal into a personal handbook of exploration and introspection. Each day, you might reflect on the rituals performed, noting what worked and what didn't. Did you feel a surge of energy during that candle spell, or was the full moon meditation surprisingly calming? Jot these observations down, along with any adjustments you might consider for next time. Your journal becomes a map, charting the course of your magical endeavors. Intention progress is another area to explore. Document how your intentions evolve over time, what obstacles you encounter, and the insights gained along the way. Think of it as a conversation with your future self, sharing wisdom and guidance that only you can offer.

Regular review of your journal entries is where the magic of growth truly happens. Set aside time each week to sit with your journal and delve into its pages. As you read through your entries, you might notice patterns emerging, like recurring themes or challenges. These patterns hold the key to deeper understanding and growth. Perhaps you discover that your energy peaks during certain moon phases, or that particular rituals resonate more deeply. Insights like these can guide your future practice, allowing you to refine and enhance your magic. Weekly review sessions can be as simple as curling up in a cozy chair with a cup of tea, flipping through the pages, and letting your thoughts wander where they will. It's a time for reflection and discovery, a moment to celebrate the journey and the person you're becoming.

Analyzing patterns and insights from your journal can be a revelatory experience. It's like piecing together a puzzle, each entry a clue that brings you closer to understanding your magical path.

Over time, you might see how certain emotions influence your practice or how external factors like the changing seasons affect your energy. These realizations are not just interesting; they're transformative, offering a deeper connection to your inner self and the world around you. As you engage with your journal, you're not just recording your experiences; you're crafting a narrative of growth and exploration. Each entry is a stepping stone, guiding you toward a richer, more fulfilling magical practice.

A magic journal is more than just a collection of words and thoughts; it's a living record of your journey, a space where your magic comes to life on the page. Through the act of journaling, you create a dialogue with yourself, one that fosters reflection, growth, and a deeper understanding of your magical path. With each entry, you add another layer to your practice, building a foundation of knowledge and experience that will support you in all your magical endeavors.

ADAPTING PRACTICES TO YOUR LIFESTYLE

We all know life isn't one-size-fits-all, and neither is witchcraft. Whether you're juggling a demanding job, family obligations, or just trying to squeeze in a moment of peace amid the chaos, your magical practice should fit seamlessly into your lifestyle. After all, magic is personal. It should feel like a cozy sweater, not an itchy wool turtleneck you can't wait to take off. Balancing work, family, and personal time is an art in itself, and your practice should enhance this balance, not disrupt it. Maybe you're a morning person, bright-eyed and bushy-tailed at the crack of dawn. Or perhaps you're a night owl, finding your groove when the rest of the world is winding down. Whatever your rhythm, make sure your practices fit it like a glove.

Customization is the name of the game when it comes to integrating witchcraft into your life. Modify your rituals to suit your schedule and energy levels. Short on time? No worries. A five-minute meditation break can work wonders, allowing you to center yourself and recharge. These quick moments of mindfulness can be just as powerful as a longer session, especially when you're consistent. And don't forget about the seasons. As the world around you changes, so can your practices. Maybe in the winter, you cozy up with a warm cup of herbal tea as part of your ritual, while in the summer, you might prefer a refreshing walk in nature.

Time-efficient techniques are your best friend when life gets hectic. Short intention-setting rituals can be done on the fly, like while waiting for your coffee to brew or during your morning shower. These moments, though small, can pack a punch in setting the tone for your day. Consider incorporating mindfulness into your daily commute, whether you're driving or taking public transport. Instead of zoning out or scrolling through your phone, take a moment to breathe deeply and focus on something you're grateful for. This practice turns a mundane activity into a magical one, grounding you and preparing you for whatever the day throws your way.

Mindful integration of witchcraft into your daily routines ensures that your practice enhances your life rather than complicates it. Imagine turning everyday activities into opportunities for magic. Cooking dinner? Stir your intentions into the pot along with the spices, letting each stir represent something you hope to achieve. Cleaning the house? Visualize sweeping away negativity with each stroke of the broom. Even a simple task like washing your hands can become a ritual of release, letting go of stress and inviting calm with each drop of water. These small acts of intention weave magic throughout your day, creating a seamless blend of the mundane and the mystical.

It's important to remember that magic doesn't always have to be a grand affair. Sometimes, it's the subtle, everyday moments that hold the most power. By integrating these practices into your life, you create a continuous flow of energy and intention. Your magical practice becomes a part of who you are, not just something you do. This integration allows you to tap into the power of magic whenever you need it, whether you're at home, at work, or anywhere in between. So embrace the flexibility, find what works for you, and let your practice evolve alongside your life and as a natural progression of it.

5.5 TRACKING YOUR PROGRESS AND GROWTH

Let's talk about the magic of tracking your progress. Imagine trying to run a marathon but the distance and path has not been identified. Chaos, right? Tracking your progress in your magical practice is a bit like having a roadmap for your marathon. It provides motivation and insights into your personal growth, allowing you to see what's working and what might need a tweak. Tracking your successes and challenges is like putting a spotlight on your practice, highlighting areas of improvement while celebrating your achievements. It's a way to keep your magical journey dynamic and engaging, ensuring that your practice evolves alongside you. When you measure your progress, you create a roadmap that guides you, offering clarity and direction in your magical endeavors. This practice not only enhances your self-awareness but also fuels your motivation, keeping you on track and inspired.

Now, let's explore some tools that can help you keep tabs on your magical journey. In this digital age, habit-tracking apps are like personal assistants, gently nudging you to stay consistent. These apps can be as simple or as detailed as you like, offering reminders, charts, and even motivational quotes to keep you going. They're perfect for tracking daily rituals, meditation sessions, or any other magical practices you've incorporated into your routine. A progress chart is another effective tool, offering a visual representation of your growth. Imagine a chart filled with symbols or stickers representing each ritual or intention you've set. Over time, this chart becomes a tapestry of your magical journey, a reminder of how far you've come and where you're headed. These tools provide a sense of accountability, ensuring you stay focused and committed to your goals.

Reflecting on your journey is where the magic of growth truly happens. Regular reflection exercises offer the opportunity to pause, breathe, and assess your progress. Monthly reflection exercises can be a time to look back on the past few weeks, noting what's worked and what hasn't. Consider setting aside a quiet evening each month to sit with a cup of tea and your journal, reflecting on your experiences and insights. As you review your entries, you might notice patterns emerging, like recurring themes or challenges. These patterns hold the key to deeper understanding and growth, offering valuable insights into areas that might need a little more attention or adjustment. Identifying areas for improvement isn't about critiquing yourself harshly but rather about nurturing your growth and evolution. It's about recognizing where you can make changes that align with your goals and values, ensuring your practice remains vibrant and fulfilling.

Celebrating milestones and achievements is the cherry on top of your magical practice. Just like you'd celebrate reaching the summit of a challenging hike, acknowledging your accomplishments in your magical journey is equally important. Rituals for marking significant progress can be simple yet meaningful. Gratitude practices for achievements can also be a powerful way to honor your progress. Take a moment to express gratitude for the growth and insights you've gained, acknowledging the hard work and dedication you've put into your practice. These celebrations are like little pep rallies for your soul, boosting your confidence and motivation, encouraging you to continue exploring and growing.

Tracking your progress not only enhances your magical practice but also deepens your connection to yourself and the world around you. It's about creating a dialogue with your journey, one that fosters reflection, growth, and a deeper understanding of your path. Through the act of tracking, you weave a tapestry of knowledge and experience, building a foundation that supports you in all your magical endeavors. As you continue to explore the world of white witchcraft, you'll find that these tools offer both guidance and inspiration, enhancing your practice in ways you never imagined. With each step, you draw closer to a life filled with purpose, love, and abundance.

In this chapter, we explored how to develop your personal practice, setting intentions, creating daily rituals, maintaining a magic journal, adapting practices to your lifestyle, and tracking your growth. Now, let's journey into the next chapter, where we'll dive into the supportive communities that can enrich your practice.

CHAPTER 6

Advanced Practices for Empowerment

I magine standing on the edge of a bustling city street, feeling the hum of life all around you—the vibrations of car engines, the chatter of passersby, the subtle thud of footsteps on pavement. In that moment, you're not just a bystander; you're part of the rhythm, the pulse. This is the essence of energy work. It's about tuning into the unseen currents that flow through everything, including you. Think of it as learning to dance with the universe, where each step and sway is a deliberate move in harmony with the forces that shape our world. Energy work is your backstage pass to understanding and manipulating these forces for your magical practices.

Let's start by exploring energy manipulation, a skill as ancient as time itself. Imagine you're at a concert, and the music is so powerful you can feel it vibrating through your chest. That's energy in action. But did you know you can sense and direct energy with your own hands? Begin by rubbing your palms together briskly, then slowly pull them apart. You might notice a tingling sensation or a sense of resistance between them. That's the energy field you're working with. With practice, you can learn to direct this energy, like a conductor guiding an orchestra. The easiest, most common method is to use your hands to shape and channel the energy you sense, focusing it toward your goals and intentions.

Grounding techniques are just as crucial, acting like the roots of a tree that keep you stable and connected to the earth. When you're grounded, you're like a rock in a stream, steady amid the flow of life's challenges. One effective method is to visualize roots extending from your feet deep into the ground. Close your eyes, take a deep breath, and picture those roots anchoring you securely. Feel the earth's energy rising through them, steadying your mind and spirit. Alternatively, you can use physical objects like stones to aid your grounding. Hold a smooth stone in your hand, letting its weight and texture draw your attention back to the present moment. This tactile connection reinforces your stability, helping you remain focused and balanced in your magical work.

Balance is the secret sauce to effective spellcasting and personal well-being. Imagine trying to ride a bike with one flat tire—it's not going to be a smooth ride. The same goes for your energy. When it's out of balance, everything feels a bit wobbly. Signs of energy imbalance might include feeling unusually tired, irritable, or scatterbrained. It's like your internal compass has lost its true north. Restoring balance involves practices that realign your energy, like yoga or tai chi, which combine movement and breath to harmonize body and spirit. Meditation is another powerful tool, allowing you to center your thoughts and emotions, creating a calm, balanced inner world. These practices are like hitting the reset button, bringing you back to your natural state of harmony.

Integrating energy work into your daily life is simpler than you might think and can significantly enhance your sense of empowerment. Consider starting your day with an energy-cleansing shower. As the water cascades over you, visualize it washing away any stress or negativity, leaving you refreshed and renewed. This simple ritual not only cleanses your body but also purifies your spirit, readying you for the day ahead. Grounding during daily meditation is another effective practice. As you sit quietly, focus on your breath, imagining each inhalation drawing in positive energy and each exhalation releasing tension. This mindful grounding connects you with the present, fostering a sense of calm and focus that supports your magical intentions.

Interactive Element: Quick Energy Check-In

Take a moment right now to do a quick energy check. Stand up, close your eyes, and take a deep breath. Imagine a soft, golden light surrounding you, gently pulsing in time with your breath. Ask yourself: How does my energy feel today? Am I buzzing like a busy bee or as calm as a quiet stream? This simple check-in helps you tune into your energy, making it easier to address any imbalances and maintain your magical flow throughout the day.

As you explore these advanced practices, remember that energy work is like learning a new dance: it takes practice, patience, and a willingness to embrace the rhythm of the universe.

ADVANCED SPELLCASTING FOR PERSONAL GOALS

Crafting spells is like cooking a complex dish. You start with a base of intention, then layer in spices of energy, symbols, and timing to create a blend that's uniquely yours. Designing complex spells means thinking beyond the basic recipe. It's about layering intentions to address multiple aspects of a goal. Let's say you're aiming for career advancement. You might layer intentions for confidence, opportunity, and success into a single spell, each intention like a note in a chord. This multifaceted approach ensures your spell resonates on different levels, making it more potent and aligned with your goals. Incorporating multiple elements—like herbs, crystals, and candles—further amplifies this power. Each element adds its unique energy, creating a rich and balanced magical brew.

Symbols and correspondences act as the language of the universe, speaking directly to the energy you wish to harness. Colors, for instance, are powerful mood-setters. Want to infuse your spell with passion? Opt for red. Need a calm, healing vibe? Blue's your buddy. These colors don't just look pretty; they carry vibrations that influence emotions and intentions. Similarly, timing your spells with planetary influences can add a layer of cosmic power. Imagine casting a spell for communication during Mercury's reign, or harnessing Jupiter's benevolence for expansion and positive outcomes. These celestial correspondences align your magic with the natural rhythms of the cosmos, amplifying your intentions and enhancing the effectiveness of your spellwork.

Customizing spells is crucial because no two paths or goals are exactly alike. Think of existing spells as templates—guides you can tweak to suit your unique needs. Personalizing chants and incantations means using words that resonate with you. They should feel like they're coming from your heart, not someone else's spellbook. Adjusting spell components is equally important. If a spell calls for a rare herb you can't find, substitute it with something similar that carries the same energy. This flexibility ensures your magic feels authentic and connected to your intentions.

THE ART OF SHADOW WORK IN MAGIC

Imagine walking into your kitchen at midnight, the lights off, and only the moonlight casting mysterious shadows on the floor. Your mind might play tricks, turning a coat on a chair into a lurking monster. This is a bit like shadow work. It's about confronting those hidden, shadowy parts of yourself—the fears, the insecurities, the bits you'd rather keep stuffed away in a mental closet. Shadow work invites you to flip the light switch on these hidden aspects, not to banish them but to understand and integrate them into the tapestry of your self-awareness. Carl Jung, the psychologist who introduced the concept of the shadow self, believed these hidden aspects are a natural part of the psyche. They're like the behind-the-scenes crew of a theater production; not seen, but essential to the whole. Engaging in shadow work isn't about scolding these parts but embracing them, understanding their origins, and how they've shaped you. The beauty of shadow work is that it can lead to profound personal growth, unearthing strengths you didn't know you had and helping you navigate life with more empathy and insight.

Let's talk about how you can start this process. Grab your journal, a trusty pen, and find a quiet spot. Begin by pondering what scares or embarrasses you about yourself. Are there traits you wish you didn't have? Write them down, no matter how silly they may seem. These journaling prompts are like breadcrumbs leading you to understand what makes you tick. Another approach is meditation, where you can meet your shadow self in a safe mental space. Picture a cozy room in your mind, one that feels welcoming and calm. Invite your shadow self to join you there. What does it look like? What does it have to say? These exercises are about opening a dialogue with parts of yourself that usually stay silent. By acknowledging them, you're already taking huge strides towards self-acceptance.

Now, once you've met your shadow, what do you do with it? Think of it like making peace with an old rival. Integration is key. It's about weaving these aspects into your life in a healthy way. Rituals for acceptance and healing can be transformative. You might incorporate symbolic acts of release, like writing down a fear on paper and then safely burning it over a candle. Transformation can be as simple as adopting a new mantra that embraces a previously feared trait. These rituals act as bridges, helping you cross from self-criticism to self-acceptance. It's about transforming what once held you back into something that propels you forward.

Safety and support are vital companions on this path. Shadow work can bring up intense emotions, so it's crucial to set boundaries. Decide how much time and energy you can devote to this work and respect those limits. It's also a good idea to have a support system in place. This might be a friend who's willing to listen without judgment or a therapist who can guide you through the deeper waters. Mentors can also offer wisdom and perspective, having probably navigated their own shadows. Remember, you're not alone in this process. Seeking guidance is a sign of strength, not weakness.

ENHANCING LOVE AND RELATIONSHIPS THROUGH RITUALS

Imagine looking in the mirror, not just to check if your hair is behaving, but to have a heart-to-heart with yourself. This is where mirror affirmations come in—simple yet profound. You stand there, eyes locked on your own, and speak words of kindness and encouragement. It's like giving your reflection a pep talk. "You've got this," you might say, "You're worthy of love." Each affirmation is a little boost for your self-confidence, a reminder that you're amazing just as you are. Then there's the magic of bath rituals for self-care and renewal. Picture a warm bath infused with rose petals and essential oils. As you soak, imagine each droplet of water washing away doubt and stress, leaving you refreshed and renewed. This is your time to indulge, to celebrate yourself in all your glorious imperfection. It's not about vanity; it's about nurturing the most important relationship you'll ever have—the one with yourself.

Now let's talk about romance. Love is a complex dance, sometimes requiring a bit of choreography. Shared rituals with your partner can deepen intimacy and create lasting bonds. Imagine a simple candle-lit dinner at home, where each course is seasoned with intention and gratitude. As you eat, you share not just food but dreams and hopes. It's about being present with each other, creating a space where love can flourish. And for those ready to take commitment to the next level, consider a love-binding spell. This isn't about trapping or controlling; it's about reinforcing the connection you both cherish. Picture a quiet evening where you and your partner craft a spell together, using symbols that represent your relationship— perhaps a lock of hair, a shared token, or a special memento. As you weave the spell, you affirm your commitment to support and cherish one another, inviting love to continue growing between you.

Family dynamics can be a wild ride, can't they? One moment you're the Brady Bunch, the next you're the cast of a reality TV drama. But with a sprinkle of magic, you can foster harmony and understanding within your family unit. Consider rituals that focus on healing and unity. Maybe it's a family gathering where you light a candle for each member, speaking words of gratitude for their presence in your life. This simple act can open the door to deeper connections and mutual respect. Or perhaps you gather your family for a blessing ceremony, where everyone shares something they love about one another. It's about creating a foundation of appreciation and love, a safe harbor in the stormy seas of life.

Let's not forget the community, that tapestry of souls that shapes our world. Building connections within your community can start with group meditations aimed at collective healing. Picture a circle of individuals, each bringing their own energy and intentions, all focused on healing and unity. As you meditate together, you create a shared space of peace and understanding, one that extends beyond the meditation room into the wider world. Community circles with shared intentions can also foster cooperation and camaraderie. Imagine sitting in a circle, each person contributing an intention for the group's well-being. It's a powerful reminder that when we work together, we create something greater than the sum of our parts. These rituals aren't just about casting spells; they're about weaving together the threads of our shared humanity, creating a vibrant tapestry of love and connection.

In the end, rituals for enhancing love and relationships are about presence and intention. They're about choosing to engage with yourself, your partner, your family, and your community in meaningful ways. These practices invite you to pause, to reflect, and to act with love. They encourage you to see the magic in everyday interactions, to recognize the sacred in the mundane. As you integrate these rituals into your life, you'll find that love isn't just an emotion; it's an active, living force that shapes and enriches your world and all of humanity.

6.5 PROTECTION SPELLS AND BOUNDARIES

Picture this: you're walking through a bustling marketplace, surrounded by vibrant colors and intoxicating scents, the world swirling around you like a kaleidoscope. You're there to enjoy the sights and sounds, but you also want to keep your wallet safe and your personal space respected. That's where protection magic comes in. It's like a magical shield, safeguarding your energy from the hustle and bustle of the world. Protection magic helps protect your energetic well-being. It acts like a cozy blanket on a cold night, wrapping you in comfort and security. Amulets and talismans are among the most common tools for protection. These small objects are imbued with intention, acting like tiny guardians that keep negative energies at bay. Imagine wearing a necklace with a protective amulet, feeling its weight remind you that you're shielded from unwanted influences. Protection circles and barriers are another powerful technique. By casting a circle, you create a sacred space where only positive energy can enter. It's like drawing an invisible line in the sand, declaring, "This is my space, and only good vibes are welcome here."

Setting boundaries, both energetic and personal, is crucial for maintaining your well-being. Think of boundaries as the fence around your garden—keeping the flowers safe from trampling feet and hungry rabbits. Visualization techniques are a great way to create these boundaries. Picture a shimmering barrier surrounding you, a barrier that lets in love and kindness but blocks out negativity and stress. Reinforce these boundaries daily with simple practices, like starting your morning with a quick visualization or ending the day with a grounding ritual. These small acts are like watering your garden, ensuring your boundaries remain strong and healthy.

Now, let's tackle defensive spells. These spells are like your magical self-defense class, teaching you how to repel negativity and maintain personal security. Banishing rituals are particularly effective for removing unwanted energies. Warding spells for personal spaces are another layer of protection. Salt, a classic protective element, can be sprinkled across doorways and windowsills, creating a barrier against negativity.

Regular cleansing is essential for maintaining a balanced and protective energy field. Think of it as spring cleaning for your aura, clearing away the dust and cobwebs of everyday life. Smudging with sage is also a popular method. As the fragrant smoke curls through the air, it purifies your space, removing lingering negativity and inviting positivity to take its place. Sound cleansing with bells or chimes is another effective technique. The clear, ringing tones revitalize your environment. These practices are simple, yet powerful, ensuring your energy remains vibrant and protected.

Protection spells and boundaries are your magical tool kit, essential for navigating the world with confidence and grace. They empower you to engage with life fully, knowing you're supported by your magic. As you incorporate these practices into your routine, you create a safe haven, a sanctuary of positivity and empowerment. With protection magic by your side, you're ready to face the world, knowing that your energy is safe, your boundaries are strong, and your spirit is free to soar. As we prepare to explore the next chapter, remember that the magic you create is a reflection of the love and intention you bring to it, paving the way for your extraordinary life!

CHAPTER 7

Overcoming Common Challenges in Witchcraft

Picture this: you're at a family dinner, and the conversation turns to hobbies. "Oh, I'm into yoga," says Aunt Mary. "I dabble in painting," chimes in your cousin. When it's your turn, you bravely mention your interest in witchcraft—and suddenly, the room goes silent. You can almost hear the crickets chirping as everyone processes this nugget of information. In that moment, you might feel like you're the star of your own reality show, "Witchcraft: Misunderstood and Misrepresented." You're not alone. Many new to witchcraft face a cauldron of myths and misconceptions. Let's stir the pot and clear the air.

For starters, there's the old notion that witchcraft is dark and malevolent, best left to the villains in fairy tales. This misconception is about as accurate as believing that all cats are plotting world domination. Sure, witchcraft has its darker stereotypes, but white witchcraft is all about positivity, healing, and harmony. It's less about curses and more about cultivating your garden, literally and metaphorically. Imagine a magical practice that focuses on spreading love and light, like a warm hug wrapped in a cozy blanket. That's the essence of white witchcraft.

Another common misconception is that witchcraft requires you to have some sort of mystical superpower, like being able to fly on a broomstick or command the elements with a whisper. The reality is much more grounded. Witchcraft is a practice, not a genetic trait. It's about setting intentions, working with nature, and opening yourself to the possibilities of the universe. Think of it as a skill you develop, like playing the guitar or baking the perfect loaf of bread. With time and practice, anyone can learn to harness the energy around them to create positive change. You don't need to be born with a wand in hand to work a little magic in your life.

Understanding the historical context of witchcraft can also help dispel these myths. In ancient cultures, witchcraft was often intertwined with healing and community roles. It wasn't until the infamous witch trials of the 15th to 17th centuries that things took a dark turn. These trials, fueled by fear and misunderstanding, painted witches as dangerous outcasts. Fast forward to today, and for some, the shadow of those misconceptions still exists. By recognizing the historical evolution of witchcraft, you can appreciate its rich and diverse heritage, free from the distortions of the past.

Within the realm of modern witchcraft, there's a dazzling array of practices and beliefs. It's like a magical buffet, offering everything from Wicca to traditional and eclectic witchcraft. Each path has its own flavor, allowing practitioners to choose what resonates best with them. Wicca, for example, is a modern pagan religion with its own rituals and deities, while traditional witchcraft might draw from ancient folk practices. Eclectic witchcraft is like the DIY version, where you mix and match elements from different traditions to create something uniquely yours. This diversity promotes inclusivity, reminding us that there's no one "right" way to be a witch. It's all about finding what sings to your soul and makes your spirit dance.

Personal stories often serve as powerful tools to illustrate the reality of witchcraft. Take Sarah, for instance, who found empowerment through her practice. After a particularly rough patch in life, she turned to witchcraft, using rituals to focus her intentions and heal old wounds. With each spell cast, Sarah grew more confident, reclaiming her power and transforming her life. Or consider Roger, who discovered a sense of community through witchcraft. Before long, he found himself surrounded by like-minded individuals who shared his passion, each gathering strengthening their bonds and collective energy. These stories shine a light on the true nature of witchcraft, dispelling myths and revealing its potential for personal and communal growth.

Interactive Element: Myth-Busting Quiz

Take a moment to test your knowledge with this quick quiz. Read each statement and decide if it's a myth or reality.

1. Witchcraft requires you to have innate magical powers.
2. White witchcraft focuses on healing and positivity.
3. All witches are part of a secret society plotting to take over the world.
4. Modern witchcraft practices can be diverse and inclusive.

Answers:

1. Myth
2. Reality

3. Myth
4. Reality

Congratulations, you're on your way to becoming a myth-busting expert!

7.2 NAVIGATING SKEPTICISM AND SELF-DOUBT

Picture this: you're standing in front of a mirror, wand in hand, ready to cast a little magic. But then, a tiny voice in your head pipes up, "Are you sure you can do this?" This internal skeptic can be louder than any outside critic, and it often knows exactly where to hit. Overcoming personal doubts about your magical abilities can feel like a solo wrestling match with your own mind. Start by grabbing a journal and writing down those pesky doubts. Ask yourself why they're there. Ask yourself if they're trying to protect you from something and if so what is it? Sometimes, just seeing them on paper can lessen their power. You might discover that your doubts are less about your abilities and more about fear of failure or the unknown. By exploring these feelings, you can start to unravel the knots they've tied in your confidence.

But what about when the skepticism comes from the outside? You know, the well-meaning family member who raises an eyebrow when you mention your magical practices, or the friend who jokes about you joining Hogwarts. It's all too easy to feel like you're constantly defending your beliefs. Crafting a personal narrative can help. Think of it as your elevator pitch for witch-craft. Keep it simple and sincere, focusing on the positive changes magic has brought into your life. For instance, you might say, "Practicing white magic helps me focus my intentions and find peace." By framing your practice in terms of personal benefits, you offer others a glimpse into your world without inviting debate or criticism. And remember, it's okay to set boundaries in these conversations. You don't owe anyone a detailed explanation of your spiritual path. A polite, "It's something I find meaningful," can often suffice.

Building self-confidence in your magical practice is a bit like tending a garden. It requires patience, care, and the occasional weeding of negative thoughts. Start with affirmations, those little nuggets of positivity that can reshape your mindset. Stand in front of that mirror and declare, "I am a powerful practitioner. My magic, prayers and positive affirmations are real and effective." Say it with conviction, even if you have to fake it at first. Over time, these affirmations become a chorus of support in your mind, drowning out doubt. And don't forget to celebrate the small successes. Did you successfully set an intention with a spell? Did you feel more centered after a ritual? These victories, no matter how minor they seem, are stepping stones on your path. Acknowledge them, perhaps with a journal entry or a small treat, reinforcing your belief in your abilities.

Empowerment through knowledge is like having a secret weapon in your magical toolbox. The more you learn, the more confident you become. Dive into books about witchcraft, exploring the many choices of practices and philosophies. Reading not only expands your understanding but also connects you with a larger community of practitioners. Knowledge becomes a shield against skepticism, both internal and external. Continuous learning keeps your practice fresh and engaging, like adding new colors to your magical palette. Consider joining workshops or online courses to deepen your skills and meet fellow witches. Engaging with others in learning environments provides support and inspiration, reminding you that you're not alone in your magical exploration. Each new piece of knowledge reinforces your confidence, transforming your practice into a wellspring of empowerment and growth.

7.3 MANAGING TIME CONSTRAINTS WITH MAGIC

In today's fast-paced world, we often find ourselves juggling more tasks than a circus performer on a caffeine high. Between work, family, and those endless Netflix queues, squeezing in time for magical practice can feel like trying to fit a square peg into a round hole. But just like finding the perfect pair of jeans, it's all about making it work for you. Start by recognizing where your time goes. We all have sneaky little time-wasters lurking in our day—whether it's an extra-long scroll through social media or that sudden urge to reorganize the spice rack. Identifying these activities is like spotting a leaky faucet; once you know where the drip is, you can fix it and save some precious minutes for your magical pursuits.

To make magic fit seamlessly into your routine, think of it as a series of small, meaningful moments rather than a grand production. Consider quick morning rituals as your way to jump-start your day with intention. Whether it's lighting a candle and setting a daily goal or a brief meditation while your coffee brews, these small practices can have a big impact. It's about making magic accessible and part of your everyday life, not something that requires an entire afternoon and a velvet robe. Multi-tasking can be your ally, too. Imagine folding laundry while mentally rehearsing a spell or focusing your intentions as you walk the dog. It's about weaving magic into the fabric of your day, transforming ordinary tasks into opportunities for spiritual growth.

When it comes to magical practice, it's not about how long you spend but the quality of that time. A short but powerful meditation can be more refreshing than a drawn-out ritual. Focused intention-setting sessions, even if they're just five minutes, can shift your mindset and set the tone for your day. Picture yourself pausing before a big meeting, taking a deep breath, and centering your thoughts on positivity and success. That tiny moment can transform your entire experience, infusing your actions with purpose and clarity. It's the intention behind the action that counts, not the time spent on it.

Consistency is the key to unlocking the full potential of your magical practice, but it shouldn't feel like a chore. Set realistic goals that fit your lifestyle, not the other way around. Maybe it's committing to a weekly ritual or a daily affirmation. Start small and let your practice grow organically. Using timers or alarms can be a gentle nudge to remind you of these commitments without overwhelming you. Think of them as little magical reminders that pop up to say, "Hey there, don't forget to sprinkle a bit of magic today!" This approach keeps you engaged and motivated, allowing your practice to become a natural part of your life.

Finding time for magic doesn't have to mean overhauling your entire schedule or sacrificing your precious downtime. It's about making small, intentional changes that align with your life and values. Embrace the freedom to adapt and experiment, finding what works best for you. Magic should enhance your life, not complicate it, offering moments of joy and reflection amidst the chaos. Remember, the goal isn't to fit into a rigid mold but to create a practice that feels authentic and fulfilling. So, whether it's a morning ritual, a quick meditation, or simply setting a daily intention, let your magical practice unfold in a way that supports and enriches your daily existence.

7.4 BALANCING SPIRITUALITY WITH DAILY RESPONSIBILITIES

Life can sometimes feel like a circus, with you juggling flaming torches while riding a unicycle. Between work, family, and social obligations, finding time for spiritual practice might seem like an impossible feat. It's crucial to identify where your spiritual aspirations clash with daily responsibilities. Perhaps you're trying to meditate while the kids are demanding breakfast or attempting a calming ritual just as emails start piling up. Balancing these aspects involves examining your routine and pinpointing conflicts. Ask yourself where your spiritual needs intersect with daily duties. Acknowledge these intersections as opportunities for growth rather than obstacles, allowing you to weave spirituality into your life without compromising your responsibilities.

Infusing spirituality into everyday tasks doesn't require you to chant mantras while running errands, unless that's your thing, then go for it! Mindfulness during chores is a simple yet profound way to bring spiritual awareness into your daily routine. Imagine washing dishes while focusing on the sensation of water and soap, letting each plate become a meditation. This not only transforms a mundane task into a spiritual practice but also grounds you in the present moment. Consider adding gratitude practices during meals. As you eat, offer silent thanks for the food, the hands that prepared it, and the earth that provided it. This practice enriches your meals with mindfulness and appreciation, turning each bite into a sacred act of nourishment.

Creating a balanced schedule is like organizing a closet—everything has its place, and there's room for both your favorite sweater and that snazzy pair of shoes. Time-blocking is a handy tool for ensuring that spiritual activities coexist with mundane tasks. Dedicate specific slots in your day for meditation, reflection, or rituals, treating them as non-negotiable appointments with yourself. This approach not only prioritizes your spiritual needs but also reduces stress by providing structure. Additionally, prioritizing tasks can lighten your load, allowing more room for spiritual pursuits. Identify tasks that drain your energy or clutter your day, and see if they can be delegated or minimized. By streamlining your responsibilities, you create a conducive environment for spiritual growth and practice.

Fostering a holistic lifestyle involves viewing your life as a harmonious whole rather than a series of disconnected parts. It's about aligning your health, wellness, and spiritual practices so they complement and support each other. Consider holistic approaches to health and wellness, such as integrating yoga or tai chi into your routine. These practices not only benefit your body but also enhance your spiritual awareness, creating a synergy between physical and spiritual well-being. Aligning life goals with spiritual values can also lead to a more fulfilling existence. Reflect on what truly matters to you—whether it's kindness, creativity, or community—and let these values guide your decisions and actions. This alignment fosters a sense of purpose and coherence, allowing your spiritual practice to naturally resonate through every aspect of your life.

Incorporating spirituality into daily life doesn't mean creating a rigid regime of rituals and meditations. Instead, it's about finding fluidity and balance, allowing your spiritual practice to ebb and flow with your daily responsibilities. Embrace flexibility and adaptability, knowing that some days your spiritual practice may be a brief moment of mindfulness, while other days it may be a more elaborate ritual. What matters is the intention behind it. Trust that your spiritual practice is a living, evolving entity, one that grows and changes with you. As you explore ways to integrate spirituality and daily life, you'll find that the two can coexist beautifully, enhancing one another and enriching your journey.

7.5 EMBRACING MISTAKES AS LEARNING OPPORTUNITIES

Imagine you're trying out a new recipe for the first time. You've got your ingredients laid out, and your playlist ready. But somewhere in your cooking process, things go awry. You end up with a tasteless dish and a messy kitchen. Do you throw up your hands and swear off cooking forever? Of course not! You laugh it off, maybe try to salvage it with a creative twist, and learn what not to do next time. The same goes for white magic. Mistakes are not failures; they're stepping stones on your path to mastery. Every spell that fizzles out or ritual that doesn't quite hit the mark offers a lesson. Embrace these lessons as part of your journey, a chance to refine your craft and grow more confident.

Reflective journaling can be a powerful tool in this process. It's your personal space to unpack what went wrong and why, to explore your thoughts and feelings without judgment. Write down your experiences, noting what didn't work and what you might try differently next time. Ask yourself questions like: What was my intention? How was my focus? Did I rush through the steps? By examining these aspects, you gain insights that turn mistakes into valuable learning opportunities. Your journal becomes a map, guiding you through the maze of trial and error with newfound clarity.

Encouraging experimentation in your practice is like opening the door to a room filled with endless possibilities. There's an exhilarating freedom in trying new rituals or techniques, in stepping outside your comfort zone to see what resonates. Maybe you experiment with a moon phase you've never worked with before or incorporate a new element into your spells. The goal is not perfection but discovery. Allow yourself to play, to mix and match methods until you find what feels right. It's in this space of experimentation that you'll stumble upon unexpected insights and breakthroughs, turning what once seemed like obstacles into stepping stones.

Consider the stories of others who have grown through their mistakes, and let their journeys inspire you. Take Sarah, for instance, who initially struggled with casting protective circles. Her early attempts often left her feeling frustrated and unprotected. But instead of giving up, she took each failure as a cue to tweak her approach. Over time, she discovered a method that clicked, transforming her practice and boosting her confidence. Or think of James, who tried his hand at divination but found himself misinterpreting the signs. With each misstep, he learned to refine his intuition, eventually becoming a trusted guide for friends seeking insight. These anecdotes remind us that growth often blooms from the soil of our missteps, each one a chance to refine our skills and deepen our understanding.

Developing resilience and adaptability is like building a toolkit that equips you to handle anything life throws your way. Imagine filling this toolkit with resources that bolster your strength and flexibility. Include practices that ground you, like meditation or energy cleansing. Add affirmations that reinforce your belief in your ability to overcome challenges. And don't forget to set flexible goals that allow for detours and adjustments, acknowledging that growth is a winding road rather than a straight path. This toolkit becomes your ally in moments of doubt or setback, a reminder that you possess the power to bounce back stronger than before.

In this journey of embracing mistakes, remember that each misstep is a brushstroke on the canvas of your magical practice. It's through these strokes, both bold and hesitant, that you create a tapestry of resilience and wisdom. So, the next time you find yourself facing a magical mishap, take a deep breath, grab your journal, and lean into the lesson it offers. Celebrate the courage it takes to make mistakes, knowing that each one brings you closer to mastery. As you continue to embrace these learning opportunities, you'll find that your practice becomes richer, more nuanced, and undeniably your own.

CHAPTER 8

Living a Magical Life

Did you know the moon has been whispering secrets and nudging dreams since time immemorial? Picture yourself gazing at the night sky, your imagination swirling with the possibilities that come with each lunar phase. The moon, with its luminous glow, isn't just a celestial body; it's a cosmic guide to manifestation, offering a rhythm that can sync with your magical practices. The moon's phases are like chapters in a book, each with its own theme and purpose, inviting you to align your intentions with its celestial dance. From the New Moon, which heralds fresh beginnings, to the Full Moon, bursting with abundance and celebration, the lunar cycle is a powerful ally in your magical toolkit. Let's explore how you can tap into this ancient wisdom, using the phases of the moon as a framework for love, manifestation and growth.

8.1 MANIFESTING WITH MOON PHASES

The New Moon is like a blank canvas, inviting you to dream up new beginnings and set intentions. This is the phase to plant seeds of hope and desire, envisioning the reality you wish to create. Imagine sitting in a quiet space, a candle flickering beside you, as you close your eyes and let your mind wander. What do you want to bring into your life? Write it down, infusing each word with passion and clarity. This ritual isn't really about making wishes; it's about setting a course, a declaration of purpose to the universe. As the moon waxes, moving towards the full glow, your intentions gather strength, much like a snowball rolling downhill, gaining momentum with each phase.

With the Waxing Moon, energy builds, making it the perfect time for growth and attraction. Picture it as a magnet, drawing opportunities and resources towards you. This is when you take action, aligning your efforts with your intentions. Whether it's sending out resumes for a job switch or nurturing the beginnings of a new relationship, the Waxing Moon supports your endeavors. It's the cosmic cheerleader, urging you to keep going, to trust in the process. Your intentions are no longer just ideas; they are becoming a tangible part of your reality.

Then comes the Full Moon, a time of abundance and celebration. This phase is like a spotlight, illuminating all that you've achieved and all that is yet to come. It's a moment to pause, reflect, and give thanks. Create a ritual of gratitude, perhaps under the moonlit sky, where you acknowledge the journey and the gifts it has brought. This isn't just about material abundance; it's about celebrating your growth, your courage, and the magic within you. The Full Moon serves as powerful support, a recognition of your efforts and a reminder that you are part of a larger, wondrous cycle.

As the moon wanes, it's time to release and let go. This phase is about shedding the old, clearing space for the new. Imagine it as a gentle breeze, sweeping away doubts, fears, and anything that no longer serves you. The Waning Moon is your chance to reset, to embrace the ebb and flow of life, and to trust in the ongoing cycle of change.

Using the lunar cycle as a framework, you can track personal growth and reflection. Consider keeping a lunar journal, where you document your intentions, achievements, and insights with each phase. This isn't just about ticking off goals; it's about understanding your journey, recognizing patterns, and celebrating progress. Reflect on each month, setting new goals and adjusting your course as needed. The moon becomes your guide, a celestial mentor that offers structure and rhythm to your magical practice.

Incorporating astrological influences adds another layer of depth to your moon-based rituals. Each moon phase occurs in a zodiac sign, infusing it with unique energies that can enhance your practice. For instance, a Full Moon in Taurus might support rituals focused on financial prosperity and stability, while a New Moon in Pisces could be perfect for spiritual exploration and creativity. Understanding these influences allows you to customize your rituals, aligning them with the cosmic energies at play.

Interactive Element: Lunar Reflection Exercise

1. Set an Intention: During the New Moon, write down a specific intention or goal you wish to focus on for the lunar cycle.
2. Track Progress: Use your lunar journal to document your actions and reflections throughout the Waxing Moon phase. Note any synchronicities or challenges you encounter.
3. Celebrate Achievements: Under the Full Moon, create a gratitude ritual to celebrate your progress. Write down

everything you're grateful for and reflect on the journey so far.

4. Release and Reset: As the Waning Moon approaches, identify what no longer serves you and perform a release ritual.

5. Review and Reflect: At the end of the lunar cycle, review your journal entries. Reflect on what you've learned and how you've grown, setting new intentions for the next cycle.

The moon, with its ever-changing face, becomes a trusted companion on your magical journey. Its phases offer a natural rhythm that guides and supports your practice, helping you manifest your dreams and navigate life's ebbs and flows. As you align with the lunar cycle, you tap into an ancient wisdom that connects you with the universe, reminding you of the magic that exists in every moment.

8.2 DAILY MINDFULNESS PRACTICES

Imagine waking up, your mind already spinning with the day's to-do list. Before you even realize it, you're off to the races, your thoughts leaping from breakfast to emails to that odd squeak in the car. But what if you could hit pause and start the day with a moment of mindfulness instead? Mindfulness isn't just a buzzword; it's a magical tool that can transform how you engage with each moment. By enhancing your awareness and intention, mindfulness sharpens your practice, much like a lens bringing a picture into focus. It's about being fully present, letting go of distractions, and tuning into the subtle energies around you. With mindfulness, you gain mental clarity, allowing you to approach life with a clear and focused mind.

Start your day with mindful breathing exercises. As you wake, take a few moments before leaping out of bed. Close your eyes and take a deep breath, feeling the air fill your lungs. Hold it for a second, then release it slowly, imagining any tension melting away. Repeat this simple exercise a few times, and you'll find yourself anchored in the present, ready to face the day with a sense of calm and purpose. This small act can set the tone for a mindful day. It's a reminder that you're in control of your thoughts and energy, not the other way around.

Mindfulness extends to the table too. Consider eating not as a rushed necessity but as an opportunity for intentional practice. Before you dive into your meal, pause to appreciate the colors, textures, and aromas. Take a bite and savor it, noticing how the flavors unfold. This isn't just about eating; it's about nourishing your body and soul with intention. Each meal becomes a ritual, a moment to connect with the magic of nourishment. By bringing mindfulness to your meals, you not only improve digestion but also cultivate a sense of gratitude for the sustenance.

Mindfulness can amplify the effectiveness of your magical intentions. Visualization practices during meditation can transform abstract desires into concrete realities. Picture yourself sitting comfortably, eyes closed, as you focus on your intention. Visualize it as vividly as possible, engaging all your senses. Feel the emotions associated with its fulfillment, and let that energy infuse your entire being. This practice acts as a magnet, drawing your desires closer, aligning your energy with your goals. Similarly, using mantras can direct and focus your energy. Choose a word or phrase that resonates with your intention, and repeat it during meditation.

Encouraging mindful observation of the world around you can open up a new magical perspective. Imagine strolling through a park, not just as a means to get from point A to point B, but as an opportunity to notice the intricate dance of nature. Pay attention to the way leaves rustle in the breeze, the play of light and shadow, and the symphony of bird calls. This isn't just a walk; it's a chance to connect with the magic of the natural world. By observing with intention, you deepen your awareness and appreciation of life's wonders, cultivating a sense of awe and connection. It's like rediscovering the world as a child, eyes wide open to the beauty and mystery that surrounds you.

Daily gratitude practices can turn ordinary moments into small, magical experiences. Before bed, take a few minutes to reflect on your day and take note of things you're grateful for. It could be as simple as a smile from a stranger or the warmth of your favorite sweater. This practice shifts your focus from what's lacking to what's abundant, creating a positive mindset that attracts more of what you appreciate. Gratitude acts as a magical amplifier, enhancing your energy and intentions. By acknowledging and appreciating the magic in everyday life, you open yourself up to even more abundance.

8.3 INCORPORATING MAGIC INTO MODERN TECHNOLOGY

Welcome to the digital age, where your smartphone might just be the most magical tool you have at your disposal. Picture this: a digital vision board that you can access anytime, anywhere. With a few taps, you can create a vibrant collage of images and affirmations that keep your intentions front and center. A digital board allows you to update and refine your goals more easily as you grow. It's a living, breathing manifestation tool that evolves alongside you, offering endless possibilities for creativity and focus. And the best part? You can carry it in your pocket, ready to inspire you whenever you need a reminder of your extraordinary potential.

Smartphone apps have revolutionized the way we approach astrology and tarot, turning what once required a library of books and a stack of cards into something accessible at your fingertips. Whether you're pulling up your daily horoscope or diving deep into a tarot reading, these apps offer insights and guidance with just a swipe. They're like having a pocket-sized oracle, ready to provide clarity and direction whenever you feel a bit lost. Plus, many of these apps come with community features, where you can share readings and connect with fellow practitioners. It's a global coven, united by technology, where you can learn, share, and grow together.

Social media platforms are not just for sharing pictures of your cat, though they're great for that, too. They're a powerful tool for building and nurturing a magical community. By joining witchcraft-themed groups and forums, you can connect with practitioners from all over the world, exchanging ideas, tips, and support. It's like having a never-ending conference, where you can learn from others and share your experiences. If you're feeling brave, share your rituals and insights online. It's a way to document your practice, receive feedback, and inspire others who might be on a similar path. The digital realm offers a unique opportunity to create a network of magical connections that transcend geographical boundaries, fostering a sense of belonging and community.

Of course, with all this digital magic at your fingertips, it's easy to get swept away in the endless notifications and screen time. That's where digital detox rituals come in. Just as you cleanse your physical space, it's important to clear your digital environment. Set aside scheduled screen-free time for reflection and reconnection with the tangible world around you. Maybe it's a day, or even just an hour, where you disconnect from devices and reconnect with yourself. During this time, engage in rituals that cleanse your digital spaces, like organizing files or deleting old apps. It's a way to bring balance, ensuring that technology remains a tool that serves your practice rather than a distraction that hinders it.

8.4 RITUALS FOR STRESS RELIEF AND PEACE

Stress. It's like that uninvited guest who shows up at the worst times, usually when you're juggling more tasks than a circus performer. In our modern world, stress seems almost unavoidable. It's woven into deadlines, traffic jams, and those never-ending email notifications. It's no wonder that finding moments of peace can feel like searching for a needle in a haystack. But here's the secret: magic can be your ally in creating calm amidst the chaos. By understanding common sources of stress, such as work pressures and relationship tensions, you can start to address them with intentional rituals designed to soothe and restore your spirit.

Imagine slipping into a warm bath infused with calming herbs and oils, the water wrapping around you like a gentle embrace. This isn't just any bath; it's a ritual for stress relief. As you add lavender and chamomile to the water, you're not only enjoying their soothing scents but also tapping into their natural properties to calm the mind and body. Light a few candles, maybe play some soft music, and let the world fade away for a while. This ritual isn't just about getting clean; it's about cleansing your energy, washing away the stress of the day. As you soak, visualize the tension melting away, leaving you refreshed and renewed.

For those moments when you need immediate relief, guided relaxation meditations with crystals can be incredibly effective.

Find a quiet space, perhaps with a cozy blanket and your favorite calming crystal—amethyst is a popular choice for its tranquil energy. Close your eyes and focus on your breath, inhaling deeply and exhaling slowly. Let the crystal rest in your hand, its cool surface grounding you as you follow a guided meditation. Picture a peaceful scene, like a sunlit meadow or a gentle stream, and allow yourself to be fully present in that space. This practice helps quiet the mind, replacing worry with peace.

Breathwork is another powerful tool in your stress-relief arsenal. When stress strikes, try a simple deep breathing exercise. Inhale slowly, counting to four, hold for a moment, then exhale to the count of four. Repeat this cycle several times, and you'll notice a shift in your energy. This technique calms the nervous system, reducing the fight-or-flight response and bringing you back to a state of balance. It's an instant way to regain control when the world feels overwhelming.

Meditation also offers a sanctuary for a busy mind. You don't need to sit cross-legged for hours to reap its benefits. Short, guided meditation scripts can help calm the mind and foster a peaceful mindset. Consider creating a simple script for yourself, focusing on themes of relaxation and tranquility. Begin by closing your eyes and taking a few deep breaths. Visualize a place where you feel completely at ease, whether it's a quiet forest or a cozy nook in your home. Allow yourself to linger in this space, noticing the details and sensations. This practice helps shift your focus from external stressors to an internal sense of peace, like stepping into a mental oasis.

Transforming your living space into a haven of tranquility can make a significant difference in managing stress. Simple changes, like using soundscapes and music, can turn your environment into a calming retreat. Choose sounds that resonate with you, perhaps the gentle patter of rain or the soft rustle of leaves, and let them fill your space. Sound has the power to soothe the soul, creating an atmosphere of peace and serenity. Arranging furniture and decor to promote comfort is another way to cultivate a calming environment. Consider adding soft lighting, cozy blankets, and elements from nature, like plants or stones. These small touches create a sanctuary where you can unwind and recharge.

8.5 CELEBRATING SEASONAL CHANGES WITH MAGIC

Think of the seasons as nature's way of throwing a fabulous party four times a year. Each season brings its own energy and symbolism, inviting us to align our practices with these natural rhythms. Imagine spring as nature's alarm clock, waking up the world with its gentle chime, calling for renewal and growth. The air is fresh with possibility, and the earth is eager to burst forth with life. Embrace this energy by engaging in planting rituals. Whether you're sowing seeds in a garden or nurturing a potted plant on your windowsill, this act symbolizes new beginnings. Feel the soil in your hands, the promise of growth in each seed, and let your intentions for personal growth take root alongside them. It's a tactile reminder of the cycle of life, a chance to plant not just flowers but also hopes and dreams.

As summer rolls in, it brings warmth and abundance, a time to bask in the light and energy of the sun. It's a season that's all about celebrating life and the fruits of our labor. Incorporate summer's vibrant energy into your rituals by creating sun-themed spaces using bright flowers, or even sunstone crystals. These elements can amplify your intentions, infusing them with the power and vitality of the sun. Picture a midsummer feast with friends, where seasonal fruits and vegetables take center stage. As you share this abundance, reflect on the blessings in your life and express gratitude for the richness of the season. This celebration isn't just about food; it's about acknowledging the abundance within and around you.

Autumn arrives with a rich tapestry of colors, a time for reflection and gratitude. The leaves turn and fall, reminding us of the beauty in letting go. Use this season to conduct gratitude ceremonies that honor what you have received and achieved. Imagine gathering leaves from your yard, using them to create a collage of gratitude. Each leaf represents something you're thankful for, a tangible expression of appreciation and reflection. As you arrange them, consider the lessons and gifts of the year, releasing what no longer serves you. This ritual becomes a gentle letting go, a cleansing of the soul as you prepare for the quiet introspection of winter.

Winter wraps the world in its quiet embrace, a time to turn inward, to rest and renew. It's a season that encourages introspection and the setting of intentions for the coming year. Create a cozy space for reflection, perhaps with a warm blanket and a flickering candle. As you settle in, engage in seasonal journaling, using prompts to explore your thoughts and feelings. What have you learned this year? What do you wish to achieve in the next? Allow these reflections to guide your goal setting, aligning your intentions with the quiet, restorative energy of winter. It's a time to plant seeds in the mind, to dream and plan for the future.

Seasonal symbols and elements are powerful additions to your magical practices. Collect leaves, flowers, or even stones that resonate with the energy of each season. Incorporate seasonal foods into your feasts, celebrating the bounty of nature. A spring salad with fresh greens, a summer smoothie with ripe berries, or a hearty winter stew—each meal becomes a ritual, a celebration of the earth's gifts. These practices connect you to the cycles of nature, grounding your magic in the tangible world.

Reflecting on personal growth through the seasons provides a framework for transformation. Use the changing seasons as a mirror, reflecting your own journey and growth. Consider setting seasonal goals, intentions that align with the energy of each time of year. As spring calls for renewal, focus on new projects or habits. As summer celebrates abundance, nurture your achievements and relationships. As autumn invites reflection, let go of what no longer serves you. And as winter encourages rest, allow yourself to dream and plan. These practices create a rhythm, a dance with nature that enriches your journey throughout the years.

Chapter 8 has taken you through the magic of living in harmony with the natural world. The seasonal cycles guide your growth, offering a framework for reflection and celebration. As you embrace the energy of each season, you connect with the world around you, grounding your practice in the rhythms of nature. In the next chapter, we'll explore sustaining this magic, focusing on lifelong learning and the evolution of your practice.

CHAPTER 9
Sustaining Your Witchcraft Journey

I magine white witchcraft as a delicious, ever-evolving recipe. You start with basic ingredients—your trusty herbs, a few crystals, maybe a candle or two. But as you dive deeper, you discover a world of flavors and techniques, each promising to transform your magical concoctions into something truly extraordinary. Continuing your education in witchcraft is like expanding your culinary repertoire, allowing you to add layers of complexity and depth to your practice. It's not about becoming a master overnight, but about savoring each new discovery and letting it enrich your spiritual journey.

The world of witchcraft is vast, with so much to explore beyond the basics. Reading advanced literature can open doors to new realms of understanding. Dive into books that challenge your perceptions and introduce complex magical theories. Whether it's a deep dive into the history of witchcraft or an exploration of advanced spellwork, there's always something new to learn. Online courses and workshops are also great resources for learning at your own pace, connecting you with experienced practitioners who share their wisdom and insights.

In today's digital age, educational resources are more accessible than ever. Enrolling in courses on magical theory and practice can provide a structured learning environment, where you're guided by experienced mentors. Attending lectures and seminars, whether virtually or in person, offers opportunities to engage with different perspectives and ask questions that deepen your understanding. Imagine sitting in a lecture hall, surrounded by fellow seekers, as a seasoned practitioner shares their insights on advanced spellcasting. These experiences not only broaden your knowledge but also connect you with a community of like-minded individuals.

Self-directed study is a powerful way to take charge of your magical education. Set learning goals that align with your interests and passions, creating a personalized reading list that challenges and inspires you. Dedicate regular study time to explore these topics, perhaps setting aside a quiet hour each week to delve into a new book or practice a new technique. This approach allows you to tailor your learning experience to your unique needs, fostering a deeper connection to your practice. Imagine curling up in your favorite chair, book in hand, as you embark on a journey of discovery that is uniquely yours. A structured approach ensures that your journey through witchcraft is not only enriching but also tailored to your personal aspirations and needs.

9.2 EVOLVING YOUR PERSONAL PRACTICE OVER TIME

Think of your practice as a living entity, one that grows and changes with you. Imagine the difference between a bustling city and a quiet village; each has its own rhythm and demands. As you transition through life's stages, your needs and energies shift. Maybe you're welcoming a new baby, moving across the country, or simply finding that your old rituals no longer resonate. Each of these changes invites you to adapt your magical routines. Perhaps you once had the luxury of elaborate rituals, but now a five-minute meditation is more your speed. Embrace these changes; they're opportunities to refine and revitalize your practice.

Reflection is a powerful tool in magic. It's like looking into a mirror that shows not just your current self but the path you've walked. Regular reflection can help you understand how personal growth and life experiences have influenced your magical work. Perhaps your beliefs or techniques have evolved over time, reflecting your personal development. Journaling can be an invaluable ally here. Writing about shifts in your magical focus or the arc of your spiritual journey helps you track your evolution and provides insight into how you can continue to grow.

Incorporating new tools and techniques keeps your practice fresh and engaging. Experiment with new ritual formats or tools that pique your interest. Maybe you've always been curious about using sound in your rituals, regardless, introducing these elements can breathe new life into your practice, keeping it vibrant and relevant.

Maintaining a dynamic practice means staying open to change and new experiences. It's easy to fall into a routine, but the magic happens when you step outside your comfort zone. Working with others can provide fresh perspectives and ideas, enriching your practice in unexpected ways. Your practice becomes not just a solitary pursuit but a living, evolving tapestry, woven from the threads of your experiences and the people you meet along the way.

ENGAGING WITH GLOBAL WITCHCRAFT TRADITIONS

Picture yourself in the vibrant, bustling markets of South America, where the air is thick with the scent of spices and the hum of lively conversation. Here, shamanic practices have been part of the cultural tapestry for centuries, offering profound insights into healing and spiritual connection. These traditions are deeply rooted in the land and its people, using rituals that honor the earth and its spirits. Imagine participating in a ceremony where drums beat a steady rhythm, guiding you into a trance-like state that connects you to the energies of nature. Such practices remind us that magic is universal, transcending borders and languages. They teach us to listen to the world around us and to the wisdom within ourselves. Shamanic traditions invite us to explore deeper aspects of our consciousness, opening pathways to healing and self-discovery.

Moving across the globe, African traditional religions offer yet another lens through which to view magic and spirituality. These practices often blend ritual and community, with ceremonies that celebrate life's milestones and transitions. Picture a vibrant gathering, where music and dance create a tapestry of sound and movement, each step a prayer, each note a call to the divine. The use of symbols, chants, and ancestral reverence forms a rich tapestry of belief that has endured for generations. As you study these traditions, you might discover parallels to your own practices, offering fresh perspectives and techniques to incorporate into your magical work. You might find that a particular chant or symbol resonates with you, becoming a part of your personal ritual toolkit.

However, as we explore these rich traditions, it's crucial to approach them with respect and sensitivity. Cultural appropriation is a very real concern, and it's our responsibility to engage ethically. This means recognizing and crediting cultural origins, understanding the significance of practices, and seeking permission and guidance from community elders when necessary. When we approach with humility and openness, we build bridges of understanding and respect. This not only enriches our practice but also honors the traditions from which we draw inspiration.

Incorporating global wisdom into your personal practice can be a transformative experience. Consider adapting universal elements like meditation or chanting to suit your needs. These practices transcend cultural boundaries, offering a shared language of spirituality. You might find that a Tibetan chant or an African drumbeat becomes a part of your daily ritual, grounding you in universal truths. Using culturally symbolic tools with respect can also enhance your practice. Perhaps you incorporate a South American talisman or an African amulet, each with its own story and energy. These elements enrich your rituals, weaving a tapestry of connection that spans the globe.

Perhaps traveling to experience these traditions first hand would be an enriching opportunity. Attending international festivals and events allows you to immerse yourself in different cultures, witnessing rituals and practices up close. Participating in cultural exchanges not only broadens your perspective but also fosters relationships with practitioners from different backgrounds.

9.4 TEACHING AND MENTORING OTHERS

Sharing your knowledge and experiences with others is like planting seeds in a community garden. Leading local workshops or classes can be an immensely rewarding way to share your passion for witchcraft. You're not just teaching; you're creating a space where curiosity thrives and connections are forged. Writing articles or creating content for witchcraft publications can also extend your reach, allowing your insights to inspire others far beyond your immediate circle. Your words become a guiding light for those navigating their own paths, offering clarity and encouragement.

Developing mentoring relationships is another powerful way to support and guide newcomers on their magical paths. One-on-one mentorship sessions provide a personalized experience where you can offer tailored guidance and support. You become a trusted advisor, someone who's walked the path before and can offer valuable insights. Creating study groups or circles adds a communal element to mentorship, where learning is a shared experience.

Teaching is an art in itself, requiring skills that can be developed and honed over time. Designing engaging lesson plans ensures that your workshops are structured and impactful, capturing the attention and interest of your participants. As you cultivate these skills, you become more effective in sharing your knowledge, empowering others to deepen their understanding and practice.

Encourage feedback and suggestions from those you mentor, creating an atmosphere where learning is reciprocal.

EMBRACING CHANGE AND TRANSFORMATION

Life, as we all know, has a funny way of throwing curveballs just when you think you've got everything under control. One minute, you're cruising along, and the next, you're caught in a whirlwind of change. Rather than resisting these shifts, consider them opportunities for growth in your magical practice. Change is the universe's way of nudging us into new territories and challenging us to grow. Embracing change allows you to flow with life rather than fighting against the current. Use these times to reevaluate and adapt your practices, finding new ways to work your magic.

The nine vital rituals can be powerful tools for personal transformation, helping us release what no longer serves us and embrace new beginnings. These practices not only facilitate personal growth but also align your magical work with the natural ebb and flow of life.

Celebrating milestones and transitions is a way to honor the journey you've undertaken and illuminate the road ahead.

REFLECTING ON YOUR JOURNEY AND ACHIEVEMENTS

Set aside regular time to engage in reflective journaling. Use prompts like "What practices have worked best during the last month?" or "How have my beliefs evolved over the past year?" This introspection helps you gain insights into your progress and highlights areas ripe for growth. Visualization exercises can also enhance self-awareness. This mental imagery can illuminate paths you didn't know existed, guiding you towards deeper understanding and fulfillment.

As you reflect, consider areas for improvement. Set goals for skill enhancement, whether it's mastering a new divination technique or deepening your understanding of herbal magic. Seeking feedback from peers or mentors can provide fresh perspectives and constructive insights. Their outside view might reveal blind spots or areas you hadn't considered, offering valuable guidance for your development.

SETTING NEW GOALS FOR THE FUTURE

Imagine standing at the edge of a vast forest, with paths winding in every direction. This is what setting new goals can feel like—an adventure waiting to unfold. The key is to make those goals clear and attainable, like selecting a path that promises not only challenge but also delight. Using the SMART criteria is a bit like packing the perfect supplies for a hike. Your goals should be Specific, Measurable, Achievable, Relevant, and Time-bound. So, instead of saying, "I want to learn more about herbs," you might set a goal to "study five new herbs, one each month, and create a herbal journal entry for each." This clarity transforms a vague desire into a roadmap, guiding you step by step. And what's a journey without a vision board? Think of it as a collage of aspirations—a visual reminder of what you're working toward, filled with images, words, and symbols that spark joy and motivation.

This regular check-in is like tending a garden—pruning what no longer serves you and making space for new growth. It's a living document that evolves as you do, reflecting your journey and guiding your way forward.

Life is unpredictable, and sometimes the winds of change blow us off our planned course. This is where flexibility in goal setting becomes invaluable. Allow room for adjustments in timelines and expectations, acknowledging that life's uncertainties often bring unexpected opportunities. You might find that a goal needs to be postponed or modified, and that's perfectly okay. Think of it as a dance with the universe, where you move in harmony with the rhythm of life. This adaptability ensures that your goals remain a source of inspiration rather than stress, empowering you to navigate life's twists and turns with grace and resilience.

To keep the fire of motivation burning brightly, celebrate small victories along the way. Each step forward, no matter how small, is a triumph worthy of recognition. Together, these practices create a supportive framework that keeps you moving forward, ever closer to the magical life you envision.

NURTURING YOUR CONNECTION WITH THE DIVINE

Imagine waking up and feeling that gentle pull towards something greater than yourself. It's that sense, the whisper of the universe, nudging you to connect with the divine. This connection is not just for the mystics and sages; it's for you, too. It begins with simple practices like daily prayer or meditation. These routines create a sacred space where you can commune with the divine in your own very personal way. Whether it's a whispered prayer over morning coffee or a few moments of stillness before bed, these practices anchor you, providing a sense of peace and purpose. Dive into the rich tapestry of your faith. Embrace these moments and honor them as part of your path. Record your spiritual insights in a journal, a private space where you can capture the whispers of inspiration and revelation. Sharing these stories with trusted community members can also be enriching, a reminder that while your path is uniquely yours, you're not walking it alone.

As we wrap up this chapter, remember that nurturing your connection with the divine is an ongoing practice. It's about creating a dialogue with the universe, a dance of discovery and reflection. Each prayer, each moment of meditation, brings you closer to the divine essence. Allow this connection to guide you, to inspire you, and to fill your life with wonder and wisdom. This journey is yours to explore, with the divine as your constant companion.

Wonderful Witchcraft Is a Journey of a Lifetime

It thrills me to see that you have come to the end of this journey through the world of white witchcraft. I hope that this is only the beginning. A witch is a being in continuous evolution; one who grows wiser, more skillful, and more creative as the years go by. As she ages, her experience and know-how grow in leaps and bounds, and her collection of rituals and practices becomes richer and more defined.

The last few pages of this book revealed the wonderful global witchcraft traditions you can embrace on your travels and take back home with you. I encourage you to embrace change and transformation; to utilize the nine vital rituals in this book to release what no longer serves you and embrace new beginnings. I also urge you to form a supportive community of witches. There is nothing like the sense of embracing transformation in the company of like-minded individuals. Take the first step toward reaching more people just like you simply by leaving a short review. Let them know that they can embrace white witchcraft in their daily lives, even if they have never dabbled in this art before.

Thanks for letting others know that it is possible to grow in wisdom, kindness, and love through white witchcraft!

Scan the QR code below

Conclusion

Well, my friend, here we are in a pause in our enchanting journey together. As you've explored the pages of this book, we've delved into the magical world of white witchcraft and discovered its harmonious dance with major world religions. This journey isn't just about casting spells or aligning crystals; it's about embracing a lifestyle imbued with love and respect.

Let's take a moment to revisit the path we've walked. You've learned how white magic can integrate seamlessly with your faith, whether it's through prayer, sacred symbols, or the mindful use of natural elements like herbs and crystals. Each chapter has offered you tools to create a life filled with love, happiness, and abundance. Use the nine practices as a stepping stone, a foundation upon which to build your extraordinary existence. Engage with like-minded communities, share your experiences, and continue to grow.

Remember, the transformative power of magic lies in intentional living. Whether it's setting intentions with the rising sun or wrapping yourself in the comforting cloak of mindfulness, these practices are your daily companions. Love, as our guiding light, expands and enriches everything it touches. It's the secret ingredient in every ritual, every spell, and every act of kindness. It's the only energy I know that grows and expands, as it is given away; and that includes both the giver and receiver. As you've journeyed through this time we have spent together, I hope you've felt the shifts in your life—those moments where magic and reality intertwine.

For a moment, reflect on your personal growth. Think about the small victories and insights gained. Whatever it may be, your journey is uniquely yours, it is a testament to your personal power and the power of exploration and growth. I encourage you to continue exploring, to let curiosity lead you deeper into the mysteries of white witchcraft and spirituality and most of all an authentic love for yourself.

Until we meet again, I want to express my heartfelt gratitude. Thank you for allowing me to join you on this path. Your openness and willingness to explore the realm of white witchcraft is deeply appreciated. It's readers like you who inspire me to continue sharing my passion for spirituality, personal growth and the manifestation of greater love in the world.

Across this space and time, that seem to separate us, I now send you my highest energy as my gift to you to live in harmony with yourself, others, and the divine, and to make your life extraordinary. Together, we can foster a nurturing community where love and understanding flourish all around this little blue planet we all call home.

Until our paths cross again, here's to an extraordinary life filled with love, happiness, and endless possibilities.

References

A Brief History of White Magic, Part 1. - *Tetragrammaton* https://www.tetragrammaton.com/content/historyofwhitemagic1

White magic - Wikipedia https://en.wikipedia.org/wiki/White_magic

A Historical Analysis of the Wiccan Rede - Project MUSE https://muse.jhu.edu/article/609097/summary

Witchcraft And Christianity: An Intriguing Intersection https://wiccanow.com/witchcraft-and-christianity-an-intriguing-intersection/

How some 'Jewitches' embrace both Judaism and witchcraft https://apnews.com/article/religion-judaism-aa34f2501659dfb3a31ca5956860ebc5

Understanding Christianity Through Magical Objects https://www.ucpress.edu/blog-posts/65587-understanding-christianity-through-magical-objects

Exploring the Similarities between Mindfulness and Witchcraft https://notquitesuperhuman.com/2023/05/22/exploring-the-similarities-between-mindfulness-and-witchcraft/

Wicca | Definition, History, Beliefs, & Facts https://www.britannica.com/topic/Wicca

White magic https://en.wikipedia.org/wiki/White_magic

Herbs that can boost your mood and memory https://newsroom.northumbria.ac.uk/pressreleases/herbs-that-can-boost-your-mood-and-memory-1389825

A Guide to Ethically Sourcing Crystals https://naturallymodernlife.com/a-guide-to-ethically-sourcing-crystals/

Article: Sustainable Witchcraft: Green Spells and Rituals https://www.llewellyn.com/journal/article/1952?srsltid=AfmBOoo-s8oW-GLEXrf41PNZs3nN-4JMpHpKbBGf6J3UC65AUi83Cx5

How To Set A Clear, Powerful Intention & Why It's Important https://theoccultwitch.com/blog/how-to-set-a-clear-powerful-intention-why-its-important

Daily Rituals Cultivate Lasting Love https://ifstudies.org/blog/daily-rituals-cultivate-lasting-love

The Importance of Keeping A Magical Journal https://horusbehdet.com/resources/the-importance-of-keeping-a-magical-journal/

Modern Witchcraft for Busy Lives: Weaving Magic into Your ... https://www.citywitch.co.uk/modern-witchcraft/

Finding Your Coven - Rebecca Beattie https://www.rebeccabeattie.co.uk/post/finding-your-coven

22 Best Spirituality communities to join in 2024 https://thehiveindex.com/topics/spirituality/

Casting a Circle in Pagan Rituals https://www.learnreligions.com/how-to-cast-a-circle-2562859

Conflict Resolution and Religion https://mediate.com/conflict-resolution-and-religion/

Five witchcraft myths debunked by an expert https://theconversation.com/five-witchcraft-myths-debunked-by-an-expert-216028

Witchcraft | Definition, History, Trials, Witch Hunts, & Facts https://www.britannica.com/topic/witchcraft

Balancing Work and Spiritual Life - Ananda.org https://www.ananda.org/blog/balancing-work-spiritual-life/

How To Build Confidence In Your Magical Abilities https://teaandrosemary.com/how-to-build-confidence-in-your-magical-abilities/

Magical Energy Manipulation and Techniques https://www.kpl.gov/catalog/item/?i=ent:/ERC_215_8682/0/215_8682:HOOPLA:13368376

How To Write A Spell Or A Ritual: A Basic Formula For Magic https://www.patheos.com/blogs/starlight/2021/02/how-to-write-a-spell-a-basic-formula-for-magic/

Shadow Work: Benefits, How To, Practices, & Dangers https://www.healthline.com/health/mental-health/shadow-work

5 Rituals to Reconnect in Your Relationship https://www.gottman.com/blog/5-rituals-reconnect-relationship/

Moon Magic: The Impact of the Lunar Cycle on ... https://www.centreofexcellence.com/moon-magic-impact-lunar-cycle-magical-activities/

Mindfulness exercises https://www.mayoclinic.org/healthy-lifestyle/consumer-health/in-depth/mindfulness-exercises/art-20046356

Exploring the intersections between religion and modern tech https://religionlink.com/source-guides/spiritual-technologies-exploring-the-intersections-between-religion-and-modern-tech/

Wheel of the Year https://en.wikipedia.org/wiki/Wheel_of_the_Year

The Temple Mystery School https://templeofwitchcraft.org/education/

Witchcraft | Definition, History, Trials, Witch Hunts, & Facts https://www.britannica.com/topic/witchcraft

The Sharpen Guide to Spiritual Mentoring https://spu.edu/depts/um/resources/downloadcenter/documents/SharpenGuidetoSpiritualMentoring09.pdf

Researcher examines relationship between the occult and ... https://www.psu.edu/news/research/story/researcher-examines-relationship-between-occult-and-religion

Smith, Erika W. and Briannah Rivera. 2023. "These 47 Witch Quotes Are Actually Magic." Cosmopolitan. August 16, 2023. https://www.cosmopolitan.com/lifestyle/a35302526/best-witch-quotes/

Made in United States
Orlando, FL
01 December 2024

54579961R00086